I0521152

DON'T TAKE THE BAIT

THE SILENT TRAP THAT REWIRES YOUR BRAIN
AND
BLOCKS YOUR DESTINY

by Amanda V.Hill

KEYSTOBALANCE
PUBLISHING

Copyright

Don't Take the Bait: The Silent Trap That Rewires Your Brain and Blocks Your Destiny

Copyright © 2025 by Amanda V. Hill

All rights reserved.

No part of this book may be reproduced, distributed, or transmitted in any form or by any means—electronic, mechanical, photocopying, recording, or otherwise—without the prior written permission of the author, except in the case of brief quotations embodied in critical articles or reviews.

Scripture quotations are taken from the Holy Bible, New International Version® (NIV), unless otherwise noted. Copyright © 1973, 1978, 1984, 2011 by Biblica, Inc.® Used by permission. All rights reserved worldwide.

This book is a work of nonfiction based on the author's personal experiences, research, and reflections. While every effort has been made to ensure accuracy, the author and publisher assume no responsibility for errors or omissions. The information provided is not intended as professional advice and should not replace consultation with qualified professionals.

Cover Design: Amanda V. Hill

Edited by: Keystobalance publishing

Published by: *Keystobalance Publishing*

ISBN: 979-8-9935112-0-7

For more information, visit:

www.keystobalance.net

or follow @AmandaVHill on social media.

All rights reserved. Printed in the United States of America.

BOOKS ALSO BY AMANDA V. HILL

THE FAITH WITHIN ME: LESSONS LEARNED THROUGH TIMES OF TRIAL

THE POWER OF THE "F" WORD IN THE WORKPLACE

YOUR ROADMAP TO SUCCESS: 5 STRATEGIES FOR GOAL ATTAINMENT

Table of Contents

FOREWORD

When Amanda first asked me to read the manuscript for *Don't Take the Bait*, I had no idea how personally it would speak to me. As an executive coach and psychologist, I've spent years studying human behavior, emotional regulation, and the intricate ways our minds process trauma and healing. But this book offered something I hadn't encountered before: a seamless integration of neuroscience, biblical wisdom, and raw, lived experience that doesn't just inform—it transforms.

Amanda's central thesis is both simple and profound: offense is not just an emotion we feel in the moment. It's a trap that literally rewires our brains, creating neural pathways that keep us stuck in cycles of bitterness, defensiveness, and pain. When we take the bait of offense, we don't just carry hurt feelings — we carry a weight that blocks our creativity, our relationships, our health, and ultimately, our destiny. What makes this book remarkable is how Amanda demonstrates that forgiveness isn't merely a spiritual obligation or a moral virtue. It's a neurological necessity. Every time we choose to forgive, we're actively rewiring our brains, building new pathways of resilience, peace, and emotional intelligence.

I know this truth intimately because I lived it. Just as Amanda was writing this book, I was navigating one of the most painful seasons of my professional life. After years of dedication to a company, I found myself on the receiving end of treatment that was not just unfair — it

THE BAIT OF OFFENSE

Why Not Taking the Bait Matters

Every single day, you and I are given opportunities to take the bait of offense. It might be a critical comment at work, a dismissive tone from a loved one, a post on social media, or even a memory from the past that replays in your mind. Offense is everywhere. And it doesn't just show up in big betrayals or painful wounds—it hides in small, subtle moments that seem harmless at first. But the truth is this: offense is not just an emotion. It's a trap.

When you take the bait of offense, you don't just carry hurt feelings. You carry heaviness, bitterness, and division. It pulls you out of your God-given identity and into a cycle of blame, defensiveness, and regret. That's why this book matters. Because the bait of offense doesn't just affect how you feel in the moment—it can shape the entire trajectory of your life if you let it.

But here's the good news: you don't have to take the bait. You can choose a different path. A path of forgiveness, freedom, and growth. And when you do, everything changes—your relationships, your health, your leadership, even the way your brain is wired.

A Quick Neuroscience + Faith Explanation of Offense

From a faith perspective, offense is spiritual warfare. Jesus warned us that offenses will come (Luke 17:1). It's not a matter of *if*, but *when*. The enemy uses offense as bait because he knows it keeps us stuck in cycles of anger, shame, and disconnection. Offense clouds our vision so we can't see clearly, and it hardens our hearts so we can't love freely.

From a neuroscience perspective, offense activates the brain's threat system. The amygdala—the part of your brain that scans for danger—lights up the moment you feel dismissed, criticized, or rejected. Your nervous system interprets offense as a threat, and suddenly, your body responds with stress hormones like cortisol and adrenaline. Over time, if left unchecked, your brain starts wiring itself around these repeated responses. Offense becomes your default mode.

This is why the Bible and neuroscience agree on something powerful: what you meditate on shapes you. Proverbs 23:7 says, *"As a man thinks in his heart, so is he."* Neuroscience confirms it— neurons that fire together, wire together. The more you rehearse offense, the more automatic it becomes. But the opposite is also true: when you rehearse forgiveness, gratitude, and truth, your brain literally rewires toward freedom and peace.

How Offense Literally Rewires the Brain and Blocks You

Here's the sobering reality: offense doesn't just hurt your feelings—it changes your brain. Every time you replay the story of how someone hurt you, your brain strengthens that neural pathway. Over time, you train your mind to live in defense, suspicion, and anger. It becomes harder to trust, harder to connect, and harder to dream.

Offense blocks creativity because your brain is stuck in survival mode. It blocks intimacy because you're too guarded to let love in. It blocks opportunity because you're too focused on what someone said about you to step boldly into your calling. In short, offense builds invisible prisons in the mind, locking you into the past while keeping you from the future God has for you.

But here's the hope: forgiveness is the key that unlocks the prison door. When you forgive, you break the cycle. You disrupt the old neural pathways and begin to form new ones rooted in grace and truth. Spiritually, you disarm the enemy and reclaim your authority. Neurologically, you create space for healing, growth, and possibility.

That's why this book exists. *Don't Take the Bait* is more than a message — it's a movement. A movement to rise above offense, to rewire your brain with forgiveness, and to walk in the fullness of who God created you to be.

The idea for this book was first planted in my heart during a speaking engagement, where I delivered a talk on leading from a position of offense. To illustrate, I gave a simple but powerful example:

Imagine you're applying for a new position within your company. You've worked hard, you're excited about the possibility, and then you overhear colleagues talking about you. Maybe you catch them saying, *"She's not ready for that role. Her presentations aren't strong enough. She doesn't have the knowledge to succeed."*

In that moment, you're faced with a decision. Do you take offense? Do you run to your friends, complain about how unfair it is, and say, *"I don't want to work with that team anyway."* Or do you pause and ask yourself, *"Is there any truth in what they're saying? Are there areas I could sharpen and grow?"* Then, instead of shutting down, you rise up, develop yourself, and still apply for the role— fully aware that you'll one day have to work with the very people who doubted you.

Both responses begin with the same scenario, but the outcomes couldn't be more different. One path leads with a spirit of offense. The other chooses forgiveness, humility, and understanding. One keeps you stuck in frustration and resentment, while the other propels you forward into development and growth. One closes doors. The other opens them wide.

Here's the truth: leading from offense doesn't just block opportunities — it stunts your growth. It robs you of becoming the best version of yourself. Offense tricks you into staying small, safe, and resentful, instead of stretching past your comfort zone and stepping into your destiny.

But this book goes far beyond workplace scenarios. Offense shows up everywhere. It sneaks into family relationships, blocking authentic connections. It shows up in marriages and dating, and breeding division instead of unity. It even creeps into your health and wellness, where self-offense whispers lies of shame and perfectionism. And in today's digital world, it shows up daily on social media—where one post, one comment, or one disagreement can spark cycles of comparison, bitterness, and anger that bleed into your personal life.

The reality is this: offense is not just a feeling — it's a trap. And if you take the bait, it will slowly shape the way you think, speak, and lead. But when you choose forgiveness, you break that cycle. You reclaim your power.

The goal of this book is simple yet transformational: to equip you with practical tools and daily practices that strengthen your "unoffendable muscle." You will learn not only how to recognize the bait of offense, but also how to release it, reframe it, and replace it with the power of forgiveness.

Because forgiveness doesn't just free the other person—it frees you. It allows you to move forward with clarity, courage, and strength.

Ultimately, this book is an invitation. An invitation to step off the hamster wheel of offense and step into a life of freedom. An invitation to lead with wisdom, grace, and resilience. And most importantly, an invitation to experience the undeniable power of forgiveness—one decision at a time.

Part 1
UNDERSTANDING THE TRAP

CHAPTER 1

THE SILENT TRAP

What Offense Is and Why It's So Dangerous

Offense is one of the enemy's most subtle traps because it doesn't always announce itself with anger or drama. Sometimes, it enters quietly — through a misunderstanding, an unmet expectation, or a careless word. It hides behind "I'm fine," while inside, something begins to shift. That tiny seed of offense, if not uprooted, will grow into resentment, bitterness, and separation.

At its core, offense is the moment we decide to hold on to what hurt us instead of releasing it to God. It's when we let pain take the lead in our perception. The real danger is not just in the feeling — it's in what that feeling begins to create within us. Offense builds invisible walls. It isolates us from the very people who could help us heal. It distorts our spiritual vision until we can no longer see others through love but only through pain. Jesus knew this, which is why He said in Luke 17:1, "It is impossible that no offenses should come." He didn't say if — He said when. Because offense isn't optional; it's inevitable. But being trapped by it is a choice.

When you take the bait of offense, you unknowingly enter into a silent agreement with bondage. You hand the enemy a blueprint of your emotional triggers and give him access to your peace. That's why it's called the silent trap — it doesn't destroy you overnight. It slowly alters your focus, drains your joy, and eventually reshapes the direction of your life.

How It Rewires Your Brain and Affects Your Future

Science now proves what Scripture has always revealed: the way you think consistently rewires the brain. When you hold on to offense, your brain begins to adapt to that emotional state.

Each time you replay the story, your brain releases stress chemicals — cortisol and adrenaline — preparing you to "defend" yourself. Over time, your neural pathways start to expect conflict, disappointment, and betrayal. You become neurologically trained to anticipate pain instead of peace.

This is where Hebb's Law comes into play — the principle that "neurons that fire together wire together." The more you meditate on the hurt, the more those thoughts strengthen their connection. What was once a single painful moment becomes a mental stronghold — a repetitive pattern that shapes your perception of yourself, others, and even God.

Spiritually, this looks like unforgiveness; neurologically, it looks like a rewired brain. Either way, the result is the same — you lose the ability to walk freely into your future. Your brain begins to build its world around the pain rather than the promise.

That's why healing isn't just emotional; it's neurological. When you forgive, when you release, when you renew your mind — you are literally building *new neural pathways*. You're teaching your brain to respond to peace, love, and compassion instead of defense and fear. Forgiveness is not weakness — it's rewiring.

Foundational Scripture and Neuroscience Insight

The Word of God gives us a clear blueprint for what modern science now calls neuroplasticity. Romans 12:2 says, "Be transformed by the renewing of your mind." That's not just poetic language — it's divine instruction for how transformation happens in the brain.

Renewing the mind means intentionally shifting what you meditate on. It means trading the story that hurts you for the truth that heals you. Every time you choose to forgive, to pray instead of replay, to bless instead of blame — you're activating a new circuit of healing.

Philippians 4:8 gives us the practical neuroscience of peace:

"Whatever is true, whatever is noble, whatever is right, whatever is pure… think on these things."

God knew that our thoughts don't just float — they form. They form emotional responses, behavioral patterns, and ultimately, our destiny. So, when you choose not to take the bait of offense, you are choosing to protect your brain, your peace, and your future.

You are saying, "I will not let this pain program me. I will let God rewire me." That's the beginning of true freedom — when you stop feeding the trap and start renewing your mind.

Choosing Freedom Over Familiar Pain

Every trap has one thing in common — bait. And offense is no different. It looks appealing in the moment because it feels justified. You were wronged. You were misunderstood. You didn't deserve what happened. And somewhere in the back of your mind, holding on to that pain feels like the only form of justice you have left.

But the problem with offense is that it keeps you emotionally tied to the very moment you want to escape. It's like trying to move forward while dragging an anchor. Every new opportunity, every new relationship, every new season becomes filtered through an old wound. You can change your scenery, but not your story — because your brain is still wired to replay it.

That's the silent part of the trap. It doesn't always show up as rage or bitterness; sometimes it's just a quiet distance, a subtle wall, or a voice in your head that whispers, *"I'll never let that happen again."* That voice feels protective, but in reality; it's a barrier to connection. It stops you from trusting again, loving fully, and walking in the divine freedom God designed for you.

Offense convinces you that closing off your heart will keep you safe, but neuroscience and Scripture agree — closing your heart also closes your capacity to grow. When your brain stays in defense mode, your body remains in a constant state of alertness. Stress hormones flood your system, keeping you tired, distracted, and reactive.

Spiritually, that looks like frustration. Physically, that looks like burnout. Emotionally, that looks like distance.

This is why forgiveness and renewal aren't just moral instructions — they are divine interventions designed to heal the brain and restore peace to the soul. Every time you choose to forgive, you interrupt that stress pattern. You stop feeding the same neural circuits of pain and begin wiring new ones of healing and peace.

Forgiveness doesn't erase the memory — it rewires your relationship with it. You no longer relive the pain; you remember the lesson. You no longer react; you respond. You no longer carry the wound; you carry the wisdom.

God, in His infinite wisdom, knew our brains could change. That's why He commanded us to *renew our minds*. He wasn't telling us to ignore reality — He was giving us the blueprint to reshape it. When you renew your mind, you're not pretending the hurt didn't happen. You're refusing to let it define your future.

There's a deep and beautiful truth in this: **you can't be transformed by what you refuse to release.** As long as offense holds space in your heart, transformation will feel distant. The Holy Spirit can't fill a vessel that's already occupied with bitterness. But when you release the offense

24

— when you give God the space to heal what hurt you — you create room for new neural pathways of faith, love, and peace to form.

It's not an overnight process. Healing rarely Is. But every decision to think differently, to respond differently, to see people differently, is building new wiring in your brain. That's how transformation works — not in one grand moment, but in small, repeated acts of obedience.

When Jesus said from the cross, *"Father, forgive them, for they know not what they do,"* He wasn't just modeling mercy — He was revealing mastery. He refused to let offense distort His mission. In the middle of unimaginable pain, He chose peace over punishment. That's the ultimate rewiring — when love overrides the natural instinct for revenge.

As you move forward through this book, I want you to ask yourself: *What offense am I still rehearsing? What story have I told myself so many times that it's become part of my identity?*

If you can name it, you can change it.

The Holy Spirit is ready to walk you through this process, not just spiritually but mentally — to reprogram the way your brain responds to pain. You are not bound by the past. You are not trapped by what they did. You are being invited into a transformation that touches every layer of your being — mind, heart, and soul.

Choosing not to take the bait doesn't mean pretending you're not hurt; it means deciding you're ready to be healed. It means you refuse to let the enemy manipulate your emotions any longer. It means you understand that your peace is worth more than your pride.

Because the truth is — offense will always come. But the trap only works if you pick it up.

And from this moment forward, you can make a new declaration over your life:

"I will not take the bait. I will not let offense rewire my brain or rewrite my destiny. My mind is being renewed. My heart is being healed. My future is free."

This is where your journey begins — at the intersection of truth and transformation.

Where Scripture meets science.

Where the mind meets the Spirit.

And where you decide that peace, not pain, will be the pattern that shapes your future.

Part 2
OFFENSE IN DAILY LIFE

CHAPTER 2
RELATIONSHIPS — FRIENDS, FAMILY & LOVE

When you think about marriage, you might picture two people so in love they can't imagine going another day without seeing each other—or at least that's how it begins. My second marriage, however, was different. It was centered around the kids—truly blending two families together with love and excitement. And I must say, the kids were the highlight of it all: volleyball games, college send-offs, family dinners, teenage arguments, crazy little kid moments, random screaming for no reason—there was never a dull moment with three teenage girls and a little autistic 3-year-old boy. Our focus was on getting the kids everywhere they needed to be, having dinner ready, keeping the house clean, and trying to keep our heads above water.

I'll never forget one moment in the kitchen before we were even married. The youngest girl, just 12 at the time, looked at me and said, "God brought you here for me." It was such a random statement, but I felt it deep in my heart. All I could say back was, "Yes, you're right."

But this wasn't an ideal marriage. My husband and I forgot about loving and caring for each other. Sacrifices became one-sided, leaving the other person feeling unseen and unheard. Our relationship shifted from a friendship into something transactional, with heartache always waiting on the other side. One person would become petty; the other would shut down. And after certain words were said and certain behaviors shown, there was no turning back.

I can't speak for how it felt for him, but as for me, I lost myself. Yes, I still went to the gym, and toward the end, I even started writing again. But inside, I was lost—trying to forgive myself for not seeing the red flags earlier, beating myself up for getting into debt to please someone else, and trusting someone who never had my best interests at heart.

Don't get me wrong — we had good moments here and there. But this marriage was built around the kids, and deep down, we both knew it. When we finally went our separate ways, my priority was to reassure the girls that I wasn't leaving them. I wanted them to know that even though I was leaving their father, I would always be a part of their lives.

In November 2022, I made one of the hardest yet most necessary decisions of my life—I moved out. My focus shifted to learning how to love myself again while still showing up fully as a mother to my oldest daughter, now in university, and to my 5-year-old son. Leaving wasn't easy. My heart was broken, but deep down, I knew this was the best decision for everyone involved.

I walked away from a 4,000-square-foot house into a 2,000-square-foot townhouse. I took only what I had brought with me. On my final trip out, as I was tidying up and closing this chapter, he came home. He didn't say much. We hugged, exchanged goodbyes, and that was it. No scene. No drama.

I had already made up my mind to keep the peace. I left with grace, love, and respect—because I wanted to model for my children that breakups don't have to be filled with chaos and theatrics. Even when there's infidelity, lies, or betrayal, you still have the power to choose how you exit. I chose to walk away with dignity and grace.

I KEPT MY WORD

I continued to visit with the girls regularly. They would come over, and we'd have our girl time — doing their hair, cooking together, watching movies, and enjoying all the little things we had always done. When Christmas came the following month, I went over that morning to exchange gifts. We spent the day as a family, and in my heart, I knew I had made the right decision. No regrets. I still had my relationship with the girls, and deep down, I knew that was truly why God had placed me with this family.

The following week after Christmas, my little boy wanted to bring his new bike over to show off. We packed it up and went over. After he finished riding, we stepped inside for just a moment, and that's when one of the girls received an awful phone call. Their biological mother had suddenly passed away at the young age of 40. This was—and still is—a life-changing moment for these girls. I was so grateful to be present when they got the call, to be able to hold and console them.

As my son finished playing, I went to put his bike back into the car, and one of the girls ran out, asking if I could take them to the hospital to see their mother one last time. I couldn't say no. I left my son with my ex-husband and drove the girls to the hospital.

When I opened the hospital door where their mother lay and heard them cry out for her, at that very second, I no longer questioned anything about my past marriage. I knew exactly why God had placed me in their lives. He knew this day was coming and that I would step up to be their bonus mom—full time. I know what it's like to be without a mother. I had accepted these girls as my very own from the day I married their father, and that was never going to change. I welcomed the role of being a shoulder to cry on, their biggest cheerleader, and their support during hard times. I've loved them as my own since day one and will continue to do so until there's no air left in my lungs.

Family has nothing to do with DNA—it's so much bigger than that. I could have taken the bait of offense, cut everything off, and started over from scratch, leaving the girls behind and moving on. But children have nothing to do with adult decisions, and I wasn't about to leave them feeling abandoned or rejected. Instead, I chose not to take the bait of offense. I chose to walk in forgiveness. The pain I experienced in that relationship was only as temporary as I allowed it to be. I decided not to ruminate on the past but to focus on the good things.

What happened between me and their father pales in comparison to the blessings that came from my relationship with these girls. I will continue to stand in the gap for them, showing them what love truly looks like and how not to walk in offense. Now, years later, our mother-daughter relationship is even stronger. God had a plan all along—but I had to make the decision not to take the bait and miss out on what truly matters: love.

Looking back, I see how easy it would have been to take the bait—to walk away bitter, offended, and resentful, convincing myself that I had been wronged beyond repair. But offense is a thief. It blinds you from your purpose, steals your peace, and robs you of the blessings hidden in unexpected places. By refusing to take the bait, I didn't just preserve a relationship with the girls; I preserved my own heart. I gained a deeper understanding of what love really is — a love that transcends DNA, circumstances, and pain. A love that keeps showing up, even when it's hard. A love that forgives, even when it's undeserved. This chapter of my life is proof that God can take what was meant to break you and use it to build you. The choice to forgive, to let go, and to walk in love has given me freedom, peace, and a purpose far greater than my hurt. And that's the power of not taking the bait—when you choose love over offense, you step into a life so much bigger than yourself.

CHAPTER 2.0 REFLECTION QUESTIONS

1. Think about a time when you felt deeply hurt or disappointed in a relationship. How did you respond   did you "take the bait" of offense, or did you choose to release it?

2. What relationships in your life (family, friends, or blended families) could transform if you chose forgiveness over resentment?

3. How has holding onto offense affected your ability to see the good or the purpose hidden in a painful situation?

4. Reflect on someone in your life who may have hurt you because of their own unhealed pain. How might viewing them through that lens change your response to them?

5. If you decided today to let go of an old hurt and not take the bait of offense, what freedom or blessing might open up for you on the other side?

ROMANTIC RELATIONSHIPS / DATING

Dating can be a challenge, let's be honest, living outside of your own bubble having to interact with others, for some can be difficult. Learning to listen without having a rebuttal ready as soon as possible, if the other person is talking outside of their neck, is a skill. Rejection is inevitable in life, with that said if you want love, companionship, you have to train your brain to handle rejection, criticism and unmet expectations without taking offense. When I interact with people and we cross an intersection where the door of offense is wide open to enter, I pause and ask myself a question. Is any part of this story correct? If yes, I take accountability and try to come up with a level of resolve. If not, I try to get some level of clarity and understanding from where this is coming from. All people want to be heard. All issues flow from your heart, and how your talk reflects what's in your heart.

If someone made a remark about you and it doesn't "feel" good. Most people would be offended and because it hurts, you want to say something back to them; to hurt them. Instead, pause and process for 5 seconds. Yes, 5 seconds. Allow the silence. See how they react to the silence. And ask, probing questions. "That was an interesting statement, what made you say that"? Most people respond based on their past experiences and presume they already have the answers. Others project from their own fears and concerns.

By pausing and asking questions; as to why they ask that question, it allows them to see themselves and helps you avoid getting offended.

Now, my feelings do get hurt; however, I don't walk in offense. When my feelings are hurt, I express exactly what happened by saying, "That hurt my feelings." Whether the other person receives it or not is none of my concern—this exercise is for me. Also, let me add, I don't always have to express myself when my feelings hurt. Most of the time, I process this within my own heart and mind rather than sharing it with the other person. This way, there's no misunderstanding, and I'm not avoiding my feelings. Getting your feelings hurt is different from getting offended. Before we continue, let's break that down.

Getting Your Feelings Hurt

This is a *natural emotional reaction*. Someone says or does something that stings—maybe it's unkind, dismissive, or even accidental. You feel sad, disappointed, or rejected in the moment. Hurt feelings are usually about *pain* and vulnerability. They can pass with time, an apology, or a simple acknowledgment.

Example: A friend forgets your birthday. You feel sad and overlooked.

Getting Offended

This is more of a *mental and emotional posture* than a passing feeling. Being offended often includes *interpretation*—assigning motives, judgments, or meanings to someone's words or actions. It can grow into resentment, anger, or a sense of moral superiority. Offense is like picking up a heavy load and deciding to carry it. It lingers because it's not just about pain; it's about *personalizing the pain and holding on to it.*

Example: A friend forgets your birthday. You decide they don't value you, get angry, and cut them off.

Hurt = an emotional wound. It happens to you.

Offense = a chosen reaction. It's how you *process and hold* that wound.

You can't always stop your feelings from being hurt, but you can decide whether to let them harden into offense.

Got it, good. Now, let's continue down this road of trying to date without getting offended. As I said, I like to pause and ask questions. In the series of questions, I'm able to determine their level of maturity and past relationship experience. Man, *I wish I mastered this in my 20's, but such is life.* This also allows you to see the heart behind a person's words. Everyone wasn't raised in a tactful environment where people understood the power of words and chose to uplift you rather than using them as weapons to manipulate.

What I have noticed is that in the dating world, if someone says something that hurts you, you feel as if you have the right and have the duty to correct them. Why is that? Could it be that at one point of your life you didn't have a voice and now that you're an adult you "must" be heard? Something to ask yourself.

Allow people to be themselves and you make the decision on whether this is something you want to navigate through. You can't change anyone, we know that, so stop trying to influence them and instead try viewing things from their perspective. Have you ever thought that maybe there is nothing wrong with them or you and you two just aren't a match? If you push someone to change, you create resistance in the relationship, which can result in avoidance and not feeling safe to share on an emotional level. This pressure can turn into offense which can poison intimacy and block a healthy connection.

At the end of the day, dating isn't about perfect people saying perfect things — it's about learning how to navigate real human interactions with grace, maturity, and emotional intelligence. When you train your brain to separate hurt feelings from offense, you protect your peace and your heart. You begin to see dating not as a battlefield of misunderstandings but as an opportunity to practice patience, discernment, and self-control. The more you pause, ask questions, and observe rather than react, the clearer you'll see whether a person is truly aligned with you or not. This is how you guard your heart without hardening it—by choosing self-awareness over self-defense, compassion over retaliation, and freedom over offense. In doing so, you give yourself the gift of entering every relationship from a place of strength and emotional wholeness rather than pain and past trauma.

CHAPTER 2.1 REFLECTION QUESTIONS

1. When was the last time you felt your feelings were hurt but didn't become offended? How did that experience differ from times when you did take offense?

2. In your dating or romantic experiences, how often do you pause before responding to hurtful comments or misunderstandings? What usually happens when you do pause?

3. How do you currently separate someone's words or actions from their intentions? What would change in your relationships if you practiced this more consistently?

4. Have you ever tried to change someone in a relationship to fit your expectations? How did that affect the connection between you two?

5. What would it look like for you to guard your heart without hardening, entering dating or relationships from a place of strength and freedom rather than pain or past trauma

FAMILY DYNAMICS

CHAPTER 3

FAMILY DYNAMICS

My childhood was not the prettiest experience and to be honest I personally don't have anyone in my circle who can say differently about their childhood. At some point we all experience a level of brokenness; the question how does you view and handle your personal "brokenness". We all have experienced rejection, abandonment on some level, abuse be it emotional, verbal, physical and some unfortunately sexually. No trauma is greater than the next. Our brains filter, response, and react differently based on our environment. My trauma happens at the age of 4, when my mother passed away at the young of 35 from cancer. Leaving my father with 5 kids to raise on his own. An 18-year-old girl, a set of twins, a month away from their 16th birthday, an 11-year-old boy and little me, 4 years old.

I can only imagine the fear, confusion, loneliness, the crying for attention, trying to fill this unexplainable feeling of separation taking place inside of me. Watching my father and siblings' tears from a distance trying to figure out; in my own childlike way, why mommy isn't present. Feeling lost, acting out, as any 4-year-old would do, chasing this invisible fulfillment, trying to replace the void in my heart. Later, to only find out that this void will never be filled.

Grief — is something I personally feel cannot be fully explained. Yes, we have psychology to explain the stages of grief: denial, anger, bargaining, depression and acceptance. These stages aren't linear, and I've learned over the years they come in waves and often, unexpectedly. My entire house was dealing with grief on a different stage — at different times. As an adult with children of my own, I can only imagine my father was in a stage of "acceptance" when he made the decision to marry again. I also believe that, because my mother's clothes were still in the closet, when she moved in, he was still in "denial" and truly didn't want to let go. After 16 years of marriage, dreams accomplished together, children, houses, ups and downs, and fighting for my mom to live; of course it wouldn't be easy to move on. In a sense, moving on would be like — "leaving" her again, another separation and ultimately another death.

At the age of 6 another adult has come into my life. This adult had unhealed trauma of her own and because of her past abuse did not have the capacity to love me as her own child. From ages of 6 to 18, I experienced verbal and physical abuse from someone who was supposed to be there to love and protect me. This shaped my mind to believe that love was conditional and transactional. It developed me into a people pleaser; always trying to create peace or help someone.

In my mind, if I could add a level of value to someone's life, they would "keep" me and see my importance.

For reasons of her own, my father's wife kept a wedge between his children and his extended family, excluding the one child they had together. Based on her past offenses reaching back over 30 years within our family and her own childhood trauma. Trauma will have you stuck in your past unable to see what's truly in front of you. You will see from a broken lens and swear it's the truth.

In my adult years after studying neuroscience and understanding the "why" behind people's behavior. It helped me to let go of my past pain and show pity towards my father's wife. She was deeply wounded in her childhood and never got help to overcome those wounds. Let's discuss what happens to the brain when major trauma takes place before the age of 8 years old.

Before age 7–8, a child's brain is in a very plastic, impressionable state. Most of their experiences are encoded in the subconscious. This is the stage when the amygdala (fear/emotion center) and the hippocampus (memory/learning) are still developing, while the prefrontal cortex (logic, self-control, empathy) is immature.

Abuse at this age — whether physical, emotional, or neglect — sets a "survival wiring" in the brain, not its trust circuits. Repeated abuse triggers the HPA axis (hypothalamus–pituitary–adrenal), flooding the body with cortisol and adrenaline. The amygdala becomes enlarged and hyperreactive constantly scanning for threat. The hippocampus (memory/context) shrinks or becomes dysregulated →

harder to process experiences rationally. The prefrontal cortex (PFC) — which helps regulate emotions, plan, and empathize — develops under stress and often ends up underactive. Result: The child's brain is wired for survival, not trust.

When these survival patterns persist into adulthood without healing or rewiring, a person can mostly struggle with forgiveness. The amygdala interprets even mild conflict as a threat. Letting go feels unsafe because "being on guard" equals survival. They will become and feel bitter and hostile, because cortisol and adrenaline remain chronically high, keeping the nervous system defensive.

They will cause pain to others, because defensive behaviors can look like anger, manipulation, or shutting down — pushing away people before they can hurt you. With that comes, the lack of or the ability to love without control. The brain equates vulnerability with danger. Control becomes a way to feel safe. Relationships are unconsciously managed to avoid abandonment or betrayal.

Essentially, the "map" for love and safety was never properly formed, so adult relationships get filtered through a trauma lens rather than a connection lens.

This wiring leads to bitterness, lack of forgiveness, and controlling love because vulnerability = danger in the nervous system. This explains why when anyone would try to ask my father's wife for forgiveness or to "start" over, she would immediately get angry, and I mean angry. Yelling, screaming, and even physically attacking you. I have story after story of her acting out on anyone, not just me; in hindsight, it's sad. She ruined many relationships and missed out on so much love and friendship.

With this explanation, of how the brain works with trauma. Everyone she felt was a "threat" because in those moments, she was experiencing everything from her past pain and past trauma in that present moment.

I'm not giving her behavior a green light, but it allows me to see the root behind the behavior and focus on the innocence of the person. Understanding, she was a broken person, living life through a broken lens.

How did I manage to experience this level of rejection and abandonment and still live a life of forgiveness and love. It wasn't easy, it was truly not allowing myself to take offense. To get offended is to take it on, to wear it, to choose to walk my life from this objective. I decided to forgive and allow God to take control.

As the years went on, the distance between my father and his children grew. We all chose to stay away to keep the peace and avoid stressing him out. We understood the dichotomy of the situation, and yes, special occasions and holidays were often challenging. Still, I always knew my father loved me. I'll never forget our last conversation—the last time I heard him say, "I love you, Mandy." That final call came in 2018 when he reached out, asking me to visit. He shared how much he missed me and asked about his granddaughter, who was sixteen at the time. I respectfully told him to speak with his wife first to ensure it was okay with her. If she agreed, we would absolutely come to visit. He never called me back. I knew she said no.

He would often send encrypted messages though my oldest brother — the last one was sent in 2024, "Tell Mandy, it's not over".

In March of 2025, my father suddenly passed away. I received the call, and my heart was broken all over again. I instantly turned into a 4-year-old little girl, trying to fill the empty void.

I didn't know how I would feel when I saw her at the funeral. Would I go back to that little girl without voice and try to please her? Would I become angry and act out? Or maybe keep my distance all together in fear that I would black out, and God knows what would happen? Surprisingly, I did none of the above. I walked in with my nervous system in place, calm and cool. I walked right up to her, hugged and gave her my condolences. The look on her face was shocking and surprised to see me. She was very pleasant to me, as you would be a stranger in an elevator, or your Uber driver. I was able to give a short speech about father, share some memories from my past and thank her for loving my father.

How was I able to do this? How was I able to meet the person who stood between me and my father at his funeral and still operated with love and compassion? It wasn't by accident. It wasn't because the pain wasn't real, or the memories didn't sting. It was because, over time, I had made the choice not to live as a prisoner to offense. Yes, I prayed, and prayer absolutely gave me peace in the middle of this storm of emotions—but there was more. I had to do the hard work of managing and regulating my emotions long before that moment. I practiced it in small, everyday situations so my nervous system would know what to do in the bigger ones. Every time I chose to forgive, every time I chose not to rehearse old hurts, I was rewiring my brain—training it to respond from a place of calm instead of a place of chaos.

I also believe God, in His grace, knew this woman was not going to change. And because of that, He placed the right resources, teachings, and people around me to prepare me for this exact encounter. When the day came, I wasn't caught off guard; my spirit was ready. My heart had been strengthened not to take the bait of offense. I had learned to look beyond her actions and see her brokenness, to separate the person from the pain she caused. So when I walked into that funeral, I wasn't walking in as a wounded child but as a healed woman, anchored in God's love. That was the real miracle—standing face-to-face with someone who represented years of loss and still being able to offer a hug, a kind word, and genuine compassion without bitterness clinging to me.

As strange as it sounds, she loved my father. He changed her life, and they were married for 40 years. Her life will never be the same after losing him and unfortunately, because of the bitterness she chose, she's living this life without the love of other family members and extended relationships. She made herself believe that justifying the offense was worth it.

On the other hand, I chose a different path. I chose not to focus on my past trauma but to actively rewire my brain by refusing to take the bait of offense. This didn't happen overnight. It was a conscious, daily choice — a decision to release what hurt me so that it wouldn't define me. By the time I walked into that funeral, I was no longer the same little girl craving approval. I was a healed, grown woman, fully aware of my worth and anchored in God's peace.

I walked away from that funeral carrying only good thoughts about my dad and the great moments we had together. I didn't focus on what didn't happen or what I missed. Instead, I chose to hold on to gratitude and love. That moment became a milestone in my journey—a visible sign of what happens when you truly let God renew your mind and train your heart to forgive.

Today, I walk in freedom, not stuck in past hurts, but looking forward with open arms to what's awaiting on the other side. I've learned that forgiveness doesn't excuse what happened; it frees you from being tied to it. It gives you your life back. And in that freedom, you don't just survive—you begin to thrive, living proof that your past doesn't have to predict your future.

HOW OFFENSE CREATES LONG-LASTING FAMILY RIFTS.

We've all heard the phrase "let go and let God," but the truth is, not everyone does. And when people hold on to old hurts, it can ripple through families in ways we don't always notice — sometimes for generations.

Short story, I have a dear friend whose brother hasn't spoken to her for over twenty years because of something that happened long ago. When they're at the same gathering, she'll say hello, and he won't even acknowledge her — as if she isn't there.

Here's what's fascinating: she's not upset. She'll even text him out of the blue with a simple, "I love you," and still, no response. But from her perspective, she's free. She forgave him. He no longer has power over her emotions because she's chosen to keep walking in love, even if it's from a distance.

Yet think about this — for him to go out of his way to ignore her at family events, doesn't that suggest she still has a hold on his emotions? And what about the ripple effect? What are the cousins experiencing? Her kids and his? Is there a quiet hesitation to connect, or maybe no relationship at all?

These silent fractures don't just affect two people; they can shape the entire family dynamic.

CHAPTER 3 REFLECTION QUESTIONS

1. When you think back to your own childhood experiences, what unhealed pain might still be shaping the way you view people and relationships today?

2. How do you typically respond when someone hurts or offends you — do you take it on, or do you release it? What does that pattern reveal about your inner wiring?

3. Consider your family relationships. Are there silent fractures, like the story of my friend and her brother, that might be rippling out to the next generation? What role could forgiveness play in shifting that dynamic?

4. If you were to look at someone who hurt you through the lens of their own unhealed trauma, how would that change your perspective on their behavior?

5. What would your life feel like if you chose to "not take the bait" of offense — to live free of bitterness and walk in love, even from a distance.

BUSINESS & WORKPLACE

CHAPTER 4

OFFENSE IN THE WORKPLACE

Offense in the workplace is something many of us have experienced up close and personal. At its most basic level, the workplace is built on a simple agreement: I provide my time, skills, and service, and in return, the company pays me a wage on an agreed-upon date. That's the baseline. Straightforward. Fair. Wouldn't you agree?

But as anyone who has worked in an organization knows, things rarely stay that simple. The human element always makes things messy. Work becomes layered with promotions, PTO requests, office politics, clashing personalities, group projects, late nights, recognition (or lack of it), and performance reviews. Suddenly, those clear expectations blur. And when our expectations aren't met—when reality doesn't line up with the script we've written in our heads—offense creeps in.

That's where entitlement often shows up. An entitlement mindset—believing we automatically *deserve* something just because we want it—sets us up for disappointment. It opens the door to resentment and bitterness. And, perhaps most tragically, it can close doors of opportunity we might have otherwise walked through.

When Entitlement Meets Reality

A close friend of mine is an executive coach for a large firm, and the stories she hears will make your jaw drop. One in particular stands out because it illustrates just how quickly offense can distort perspective. She was coaching a young professional who earned around $250,000 a year. This woman had just returned from maternity leave after being away from the office for nine months. By piecing together vacation time and short-term medical leave, she had been able to stay home while maintaining her salary. Add to that the fact that her spouse also made over $250,000 a year, and you can see they were doing quite well financially.

When she returned, the company went above and beyond to accommodate her transition back to work. They offered a flexible schedule: three days in the office and two days from home, so she could ease back into the demands of a full-time role. By most standards, this was more than generous.

But here's where offense crept in. She expected an immediate promotion upon her return. The company had a set promotion cycle— once a year, across the board. Her argument was that because she had been a high performer before her leave, she should be considered for advancement now. When she got passed over for the promotion, she became deeply offended and concluded the decision was rooted in bias against her pregnancy, rather than the reasonable fact that she had been away from her role for nearly a year.

Think about this from another perspective. Imagine being the colleague who had been carrying her workload for those nine months. Wouldn't you feel entitled to be considered for advancement too?

Offense works both ways. It blinds us to context. It narrows our perspective until we see only *our* unmet desire and nothing else.

My friend, as a coach, couldn't correct her client's mindset directly. That wasn't her role. But she guided her toward strategies to keep her career moving forward. That's the bigger lesson: offense doesn't just steal our peace; it can stall our progress.

Balancing Career and Family

This story also raises a deeper question many professionals wrestle with: how do you balance ambition with family? How do you pursue advancement while also being present for the people who matter most?

Children, especially, crave time more than anything else. Yes, they'll ask for toys, gadgets, or experiences, but what they want most is attention. There was a commercial years ago that captured this perfectly. A little boy kept asking his dad, who was glued to his work, to play. Finally, frustrated, the boy asked how much his dad made an hour. The father gave him a number. The child ran to get his piggy bank and offered the money to "buy" an hour of his father's time.

That image still breaks hearts today. Many of us are guilty of prioritizing work, chasing promotions, or trying to meet external expectations—only to miss the moments we can't rewind.

56

This isn't to say ambition is bad. But when offense is driving our ambition, it pushes us into comparison, bitterness, and even strained family relationships. A promotion might look like the prize, but if it costs you your peace or your presence with your family, is it really worth it?

My Personal Encounter with Offense

I've had my own brush with workplace offense. Early in my career, I transitioned into a new department and created a process flow that was so effective it ended up being used across multiple clients. Not long after, a new manager came in. She was under intense pressure to deliver results. When she discovered my process, she included it in her presentation to executives—without giving me any credit.

I was furious. Offended to the core. My first instinct was to call her out publicly. But instead, I stayed silent. I kept working hard, prayed for wisdom, and trusted that my work would speak for itself.

Months later, I was offered a better role in another department with a pay increase and the ability to work from home. Meanwhile, that same manager casually chatted with me just days before my transition. She never apologized, but we had a lighthearted exchange. The very next day, I got a call saying she had passed away in her sleep.

That moment shook me. Imagine if I had stayed bitter. Imagine if I had slandered her name around the office or allowed resentment to poison my heart. Offense would have stolen not only my peace but also the blessing of moving forward.

Choosing Growth Over Offense

Not everyone responds to offense with bitterness. After one of my speaking engagements, a woman—let's call her Mary—shared her story with me. She had been pursuing a career in IT and kept asking a mentor for guidance. His response was always the same: "You're not ready."

She could have easily taken offense. She could have allowed those words to crush her confidence. But instead, she chose to grow. She studied the job description, identified her weak spots, and earned an additional certification. When she applied again, she not only landed the job but also received a higher salary than she expected.

Mary didn't let offense define her. She took the meat and threw away the bone. She used feedback—however blunt or poorly delivered—as fuel for growth.

The Ripple Effect of Offense

Offense doesn't stay contained. When we carry it, it leaks into everything. A snub from a coworker can sour our mood with our family. A passed-over promotion can make us short-tempered with friends. Offense is like carrying around a heavy backpack—eventually, it wears us down and spills out in other areas of life.

And here's the danger: offense in the workplace doesn't just affect our emotional state. It can block creativity, stall promotions, and poison team morale, and even damage our leadership influence. People follow leaders who inspire, not those who are perpetually offended.

Work will always bring challenges, personalities, and situations that test us. Offense will always knock at the door—but we don't have to let it in. Choosing grace, humility, and perspective doesn't mean ignoring unfairness; it means refusing to let bitterness rule. Sometimes that looks like forgiving quietly, as I did with my manager. Sometimes it looks like turning offense into growth, as Mary did.

At the end of the day, success isn't just about promotions or paychecks. True success is about impact, peace, and legacy. If you gain the whole career ladder but lose your joy, your health, or your relationships, what have you really won?

So, here's the challenge: don't let offense rob you of opportunities, peace, or influence. In the workplace—and in life—your greatest power is not in proving yourself right, but in choosing not to be offended. That choice opens doors no resentment ever could.

CHAPTER 4 REFLECTION QUESTIONS

1. When was the last time I felt offended at work, and what underlying expectation did I have that wasn't met?

2. How has offense — whether big or small — impacted my career growth, creativity, or relationships with coworkers?

3. Do I approach opportunities at work with an entitlement mindset, or with a growth mindset that looks for ways to improve myself?

4. In what situations could I choose grace or perspective instead of holding onto resentment in the workplace?

5. How can I "take the meat and throw away the bone" in my own career—using constructive feedback (even when it stings) as fuel for growth?

HEALTH & WELLNESS

CHAPTER 5

HEALTH & WELLNESS

The body is amazing. When you take time to study it from your head to toe, you can only be in awe of what God created. To understand that the lining of your stomach renews every 2 to 4 days, you get new blood every 90 to 120 days, and if you damage your liver, it can regrow lost tissue over time roughly every 300–500 days. Your body was created to heal itself in the right conditions. With the right food, exercise, rest, and environment, your body is designed to live a long, healthy life.

📑 Cell & Tissue Renewal Times	
Cell / Organ / Tissue	Average Renewal Time
Stomach lining	2–4 days
Skin cells	2–4 weeks
Intestinal lining	3–5 days
Red blood cells	90–120 days
White blood cells	1–3 days (varies by type)
Liver cells	300–500 days (continuous regeneration)
Fat cells	~8 years
Bone cells	~10 years
Skeletal muscle cells	~15 years
Neurons (cerebral cortex)	Lifetime (most do not renew)

Unfortunately, we can't always have control over our environment, and we must learn to remove stress from our life—not manage it—because stress is a silent killer. Inflammation is talked about by many, but I don't believe many fully understand how inflammation harms. We need a low level of inflammation to heal wounds, but at higher levels it will cause damage. Allow me to explain how inflammation can become a norm in your life.

Imagine you're stuck in traffic, running late for a big meeting. Your heart rate rises, your muscles tighten, and your mind starts racing. This is your fight-or-flight response kicking in. Your body releases stress hormones like cortisol and adrenaline to help you "survive" the perceived threat.

In a short burst, this response is helpful. But if you're stressed like this every day—emails, deadlines, finances, or relationship tensions—your body stays in "fight-or-flight mode." Chronic stress means:

- Cortisol stays elevated (should be temporary)
- Your immune system is constantly activated
- Your body begins producing pro-inflammatory cytokines (molecules that promote inflammation)

Over time, this ongoing low-level inflammation can show up as:

- Achy joints
- Digestive issues
- Headaches
- Fatigue

- Increased risk of chronic illnesses (heart disease, diabetes, autoimmune issues)

The crazy part is, so many people live this lifestyle on the regular that they don't know any difference. People are used to having gut issues, headaches, and fatigue and have accepted autoimmune issues as something that "runs in the family," telling themselves they can't do anything to prevent it.

People presume because I'm fit today that I've always been this way, which is so far from the truth. When I was 20, I was a size 12-14 and the weight was in all the right places if you get what I'm saying. This summer I was staying with my brother on Ocean Side Blvd. in Long Beach, CA. The mall was my best friend, and dates were coming left and right. One day I was with my brother at his place, and he said, mid-conversation, "Mandy, you need to lose 15 pounds. Women gain an average of 5 to 8 pounds per year, and if you don't fix this by the time you're 30, you will be looking crazy." I was speechless. My mouth dropped. I didn't say a word. What could I say? My brother used to be one of the best trainers in the area, he looked great, and he read about fitness all the time. At this time, I knew nothing about health and fitness. All I did was play sports and eat fast food. I didn't challenge what he said. My feelings were hurt because I thought I was cute, and he did say, "You are cute, but this will catch up with you."

I started changing my eating habits right away—no more red meat and I added more fish. When I got back to college that fall, I started to pay attention to the food I was eating and trained differently. When my mind changed, my body changed automatically. Without my brother calling me out, I would never have thought I was going down the track of living an unhealthy life because I was so young. Now, in hindsight, I understand why my gut was bloated as well as all over my body. It wasn't just because of the food, but also because of the stress I was under—trying to decide whether to go back to Wisconsin to college or stay in California, plus family drama. I have what's called a "stress gut." I hold all my stress in my digestive system. For some people, it's in their shoulders, others get headaches; for me, I get bloated and IBS kicks in. I made the decision to not "manage" it and instead fix it. So, I remove stress from my life and only eat food with no or low inflammation during challenging times. (See the Inflammation vs. Lifestyle Choices Bar Chart)

Inflammation vs. Lifestyle Choices Bar Chart	
Title: *What Raises and Lowers Inflammation in Your Body*	
Lifestyle Factor	**Impact on Inflammation**
Sugary Drinks / Soda	High ↑
Processed Foods	High ↑
Lack of Sleep	Moderate ↑
Stress	High ↑
Alcohol Excess	Moderate ↑
Healthy Foods (Vegetables, Fish, Whole Grains)	Low ↓
Exercise	Low ↓
Proper Sleep	Low ↓
Stress Management (Meditation, Prayer)	Low ↓

- Chronic stress, poor diet, and unhealthy habits silently inflame your body.

- Practicing discipline and making intentional changes lowers inflammation, protects your body, and supports overall health.

Telling someone they need to live a healthy lifestyle is difficult. Most of the time people will make excuses because change is uncomfortable, and it's easy to put band-aids on instead of tackling problems head-on and putting in the work. We live in an Amazon world now and people want a ready-made body right away. They would rather go under the knife and pay thousands of dollars for surgery instead of making hard choices and changing their eating habits and activity level.

Here's the deal: so many people get upset when you try to tell them to change their eating habits because food can be a drug. We have seen what drugs do to people when they can't have them—they act up in a major way. The only difference between someone taking illegal drugs and eating processed foods is which one is frowned upon. The same chemicals are released in your brain when you're eating that crispy fried chicken wing, delicious chocolate cake, cold soda, or your favorite pasta dish as that person taking a hit of heroin or meth. You're both chasing that first high. Both are being pulled in by stress or triggers. Both repeats the same statement, "just one more time" when trying to stop. Both parties get upset when someone tries to help them live a healthier life. Both are killing themselves. The only difference is one is justified and supported to keep their addiction up with marketing and society.

Let's discuss what's happening on a neurological level when you're trying to "get the next high" and when you're trying to stop. Have you ever noticed that the first bite of a slice of pizza, a chocolate bar, or a crunchy bag of chips taste like heaven. That's not just in your head—well, actually; it's kind of is, but in the best way. When we eat highly processed foods, our brain lights up in a very specific way, releasing a cocktail of chemicals that make us feel amazing. Understanding what happens neurologically can help explain why it's so hard to stop, even when we *know* we want to eat healthier.

When you take that first bite of something processed, your brain registers it as a reward. The taste buds send signals to your brain's **mesolimbic pathway**, commonly known as the reward pathway. This pathway is responsible for feelings of pleasure and motivation. The key player here is **dopamine**; a neurotransmitter often called the "feel-good chemical." Dopamine spikes with that first bite, creating a pleasurable rush, a mini celebration in your brain. That moment? Pure bliss. But it doesn't stop there. Processed foods are designed to hit multiple pleasure centers. They're often high in **sugar, fat, and salt**, which together form a trifecta that makes the brain release **endorphins**, another feel-good chemical. Endorphins are like tiny fireworks in your brain, giving a sense of euphoria—almost like your body is saying, "Yes! Do this again!" And because these foods are engineered to be hyper-palatable, your brain doesn't just enjoy them; it craves them.

Here's where it gets tricky. Your **prefrontal cortex**, the part of the brain responsible for self-control and decision-making, doesn't fully mature until your mid-20s. Even as adults, you must work extra hard to resist these engineered foods. So, when that slice of cake or bag of chips calls your name, your reward pathway is screaming "YES!" while your self-control center is waving a white flag. That first bite is so good because your brain is wired to survive—and for thousands of years, it interpreted fat, sugar, and salt as rare, high-energy resources. Modern processed foods exploit that survival wiring.

The brain also forms a kind of memory around the pleasure of that first bite. The **hippocampus**, which handles memory and learning, remembers how good that food made you feel, creating a pattern that encourages repeat behavior. Every time you eat it, your brain anticipates the same dopamine rush, reinforcing the habit. This is called **neuroplasticity**—your brain literally wires itself to crave that processed food again and again.

Then there's another sneaky chemical: **ghrelin**. When you eat sugary, processed foods, ghrelin can spike, telling your brain that you're hungry even if you've eaten enough calories. Combined with the dopamine reward loop, this creates a perfect storm for cravings. You don't just want food; your brain insists you *need* it. And because your body experiences a temporary blood sugar spike followed by a rapid drop, it often leaves you feeling tired, irritable, or hungry again soon after—the classic sugar crash that leads to *more* processed food.

Breaking this cycle is tough, but not impossible. The brain thrives on repetition. If you replace processed foods with healthier alternatives, your dopamine pathways can recalibrate over time. The first bite of a fresh smoothie, roasted vegetables, or lean protein may not give the instant fireworks of a candy bar, but as your brain adjusts, you begin to experience a steady, more sustainable pleasure—energy that lasts, digestion that feels better, and a nervous system less stressed by sugar spikes.

Understanding science can be empowering. When cravings hit, remember it's not a lack of willpower—it's your brain signaling for the reward it's been trained to expect. Pausing, choosing a healthier option, or even savoring a smaller portion can help train the **prefrontal cortex** to regain control. Over time, those first bites of wholesome foods become rewarding in their own way, and the hold processed foods have over your brain begins to loosen.

In short, your brain loves processed foods because they trigger dopamine, endorphins, and memory pathways, creating immediate pleasure and long-term cravings. But by understanding this, you can make informed choices, reshape your reward system, and reclaim control over your eating habits. That first bite may always feel amazing, but with practice and awareness, every bite afterward can be just as powerful— without a crash.

This topic really gets to me because I see so many people leaving the earth too soon simply because they lack self-control. We must adopt a lifestyle of discipline and make a conscious decision to no longer get offended when someone tells you to stop drinking soda or eating processed foods. Instead of taking it as judgment, see it as an act of love—a wake-up call. Why wait until something awful happens to make a change? Too often, people only act after a diagnosis, hospitalization, or the loss of someone close. By then, habits are harder to break, and damage may already be done. True transformation begins with humility and a willingness to receive

correction without offense. The earlier we embrace discipline and healthy choices, the more time we give our bodies to heal, renew, and thrive. See Feedback & Offense Funnel Chart

Feedback & Offense Funnel

Title: *How Your Reaction Shapes Your Health*

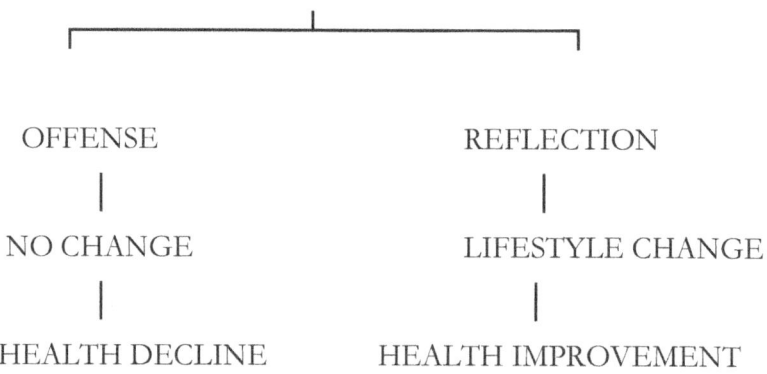

FEEDBACK

OFFENSE	REFLECTION
NO CHANGE	LIFESTYLE CHANGE
HEALTH DECLINE	HEALTH IMPROVEMENT

If you take offense at feedback (like "eat healthier" or "exercise more"), you block the opportunity for growth.

If you reflect instead, even if it stings at first, you can make real changes that improve your health, longevity, and well-being.

And here's what changed my life: I could have taken my brother's words as an insult. I could have gotten offended, shut down, or even ruined our relationship by making it about my pride instead of my health. But I didn't. I chose to listen with an open heart. His honesty, though it stung at first, was the spark that helped me shift my habits and my mindset. Today, I look back and realize that moment taught me one of the most powerful lessons of my life—sometimes the feedback that hurts your feelings the most is the exact thing God uses to save you. By not getting offended, I gained not only a healthier body but also a stronger bond with my brother and a new level of self-respect. That choice changed my life forever.

Offense doesn't just live in your mind; it lives in your body. When you hold on to offense, your nervous system stays on high alert, your stress hormones stay elevated, and your body resists healing. It can stall weight loss, keep inflammation high, and block your ability to receive feedback that could change your life. Offense builds walls around your heart and even around your health. But when you release it—when you choose to forgive, let go, and stay open—you give your body permission to heal, your mind permission to grow, and your spirit permission to thrive.

The one area where I constantly must check myself when it comes to getting offended is in the realm of health and wellness. I'll be totally transparent here—this is my tender spot. For years, I carried a lot of judgment toward people who weren't losing weight, or at least not trying to make better choices. I would quietly assign motives in my head, thinking they weren't disciplined enough or didn't care enough about their health. But over time, I had to learn to let go of those judgments. Why? Because they were poisoning my own peace.

I've been in the health and wellness world for nearly two decades now. I've trained hundreds of people, competed in NPC competitions, and experienced firsthand the power of transforming the body. But here's the truth I know deep in my bones: it's never just about the body. It's mental. The body follows the mind. When someone truly rewires their thoughts, habits, and beliefs, the body has no choice but to follow. This is why you can give two people the same exact workout plan—one will thrive while the other barely gets started. The difference isn't the plan. It's the mindset.

And mindset requires discipline. Discipline is where my frustration kicks in the most, because I know it's available to everyone. We are creatures of patterns and habits, most of which are shaped by what we find pleasurable. But let's be honest — what feels good in the moment doesn't always serve us long-term. A donut feels good. Netflix binges feel good. Sleeping feels good. But the "feel-good" in the moment often robs us of the "feel-amazing" of the future. Discipline is what bridges that gap. Discipline is what helps you see your future self and take action for that version of you, not just the version that wants comfort right now.

Motivation comes and goes—it's like the weather. But discipline? Discipline eats motivation for lunch every single day. And yet, so many people resist it. They wait until they "feel like it," and in the meantime, they're slipping further away from their goals. That's hard for me to watch.

It's a challenge to see incredible people with amazing gifts eat and drink themselves into hospital beds simply because of a lack of self-control. And what really makes my blood boil is when people spiritualize their health consequences by saying things like, "Well, God took him home," or "It was just her time." No. Let's be honest—God had nothing to do with drinking soda as your main beverage. God didn't have anything to do with eating processed foods day in and day out. And God certainly didn't force anyone to skip movement and exercise. Those are choices. And choices come with consequences.

I'll admit, it used to offend me deeply when people would ask me for advice—sometimes even beg me for a workout plan—only to ignore it completely. I took it personally. I felt like they were wasting my time or dismissing the passion I've dedicated my life to. But then I had to step back and remind myself: people aren't rejecting me. They're rejecting discipline. And often, they're not even aware that their brain is hooked.

See, food really is a drug for many people. The same brain chemistry that drives addictions to substances is at play when someone feels powerless against sugar, fast food, or processed snacks. Once I started to study neuroscience, I understood this on a deeper level. Junk food hijacks the brain's reward pathways, giving people temporary hits of dopamine and comfort, while keeping them stuck in a cycle that's hard to break. With that awareness, I began to let go of offense and replace it with compassion. Instead of being angry, I could see them as caught in something bigger than willpower alone.

That doesn't mean I don't give hard love—I still do, because that's who I am. But it does mean I don't carry the offense anymore. I don't let it stick to me or steal my joy. I pause, take a breath, and choose grace. And when I can't change the choices someone else is making, I release it and remind myself: my responsibility is to steward my own health and to encourage others without letting their decisions weigh down my spirit.

My deep frustration with this issue comes from a place of loss. I lost my mother to cancer, and years later, I watched my father suffer a stroke. Those moments marked me. They made me passionate about helping others avoid unnecessary pain. So, when I see someone willingly heading down a similar path, it hits me in a tender place. But again, I've learned that offense doesn't heal anyone. What heals is love, truth, and consistent encouragement.

Health is not just about food and exercise. It's about stewardship. Our bodies are temples, and we're entrusted to care for them. It's not always easy, and it doesn't always feel good, but it is always worth it. Because when you have your health, you have energy, clarity, and the ability to pour into your calling and the people you love. Without it, everything else becomes harder.

So, I've made peace with this tension. Yes, it hurts to see people waste their potential. Yes, I'll always feel that tug in my heart when I see unhealthy choices. But instead of walking in offense, I now walk in grace. I remind myself that change is a process. Sometimes people need years before they're ready to take it seriously. My role isn't to carry the weight of their choices — it's to model what's possible, to live in discipline, and to speak truth with love.

And here's what I've learned: when I release the offense, I make space for influence. People may not listen when they feel judged, but they will listen when they feel seen, loved, and believed in. My job is not to shame them into health. It's to inspire them toward it.

At the end of the day, offense blocks connection, and connection is the very thing that makes transformation possible. So, whether it's health, wellness, or any other area of life, the greatest gift we can give others is not our judgment—but our grace.

CHAPTER 5 REFLECTION QUESTIONS

1.How do I currently react when someone offers feedback about my health, diet, or lifestyle—do I take offense or reflect and take action?

2. In what ways has stress or unresolved offense impacted my physical health, such as weight, digestion, sleep, or energy levels?

3. What habits or lifestyle choices am I holding onto that may be silently increasing inflammation in my body?

4. How can I practice discipline and self-control today to protect my long-term health, rather than waiting for a crisis to force change?

5. Where in my life do I need to choose reflection over offense to allow for healing, growth, and better physical well-being?

SOCIAL MEDIA & PUBLIC SPACES

CHAPTER 6

SOCIAL MEDIA & PUBLIC SPACES

Did you know that historians were able to identify the first newspaper going back to 59 BCE. Although no copies of the paper have survived it was widely discovered to have published chronicles of events, assemblies, births, deaths and daily gossip. Daily gossip —you heard that right, can you imagine what was written about the local paper? "Eyewitnesses claim Julius Caesar was spotted sharing honeyed wine with a mysterious cloaked figure from Gaul. Sources say the Druid was "teaching him new magic words" — but insiders whisper it's just a new speechwriter." Or "Senator's Wife Spotted at Gladiator School — Rumors swirl that a certain patrician lady has been sneaking off to the Ludus Magnus to watch her "favorite" gladiator train. The senator denies it, but sources say she's bringing extra olive oil." There is nothing new under the sun, I hope you see the humor in this as I do.

In modern times in America, in 1704, there was the first successful and continually published newspaper, The Boston Newsletter. From the beginning of time, I'm sure there was some form of communication to influence the body of people. One may have good intentions with the purpose of only wanting to provide knowledge and educate the reader. While others' goal is to gain power and influence over others to join the collective for their own agenda. We saw this play out on a massive scale during World War I, were patriotic propaganda, government messaging, and news dissemination shaped public perception. The narrative was steered to promote enlistment, encourage national unity, and foster anti-German sentiment, with government initiatives pushing patriotic reporting while suppressing dissent. Newspapers also played a key role in maintaining morale by connecting the home front to the soldiers' experiences, while simultaneously shaping international opinion by spreading a pro-Allied perspective.

The media, from newspapers, television, to now social media has sharpened the world into what we see today. Our social structure has transformed our reality. Outside entities have shaped your desires on a large scale, influencing your decisions by gently using fear tactics. It can range from the clothes you wear, the food you eat, the places you visit, how you vote and even how you see yourself. What you consume on the daily shapes how you see the world and now in 2025, the access is right in your hand coming from millions of people from their own point of view, without any guidance or fact checks. This opens the doors to echo chambers – where you're only listening to people with your views, repeatedly on a daily basics. Eliminating access to healthy discussion with a difference of opinion is dangerous. Having a difference of opinion is healthy considering we all have blind spots and can lack knowledge in certain areas, to depend solely on one source of information in a world full of deception is foolish. However, because people are wired to want community and connection, they will join the masses in fit in and now with social media, everyone has a voice, an opinion, and comment they feel must be shared, even if it hurts another person.

Remember, we already explained the difference between getting our "feelings" hurt and getting offended. In the social media world in current day, you have Facebook, Instagram, TikTok, YouTube and more. A place where a person can build their personal brand, business, share family updates, where they ate last night, what's on their mind, and whatever other meaningless thing you can think of. Social media is used for marketing, advertising for companies big and small, politics, sports updates, per comedy relief, food and dining ideas, you name it; it's on social media.

To be an influencer on social media, you must be able to pull someone into believing in your cause on a large scale. It's not just about posting pretty pictures or catchy videos; it's about creating a narrative that feels so compelling people start to see the world through your lens. Real influence goes beyond "likes" — it shapes opinions, sparks action and builds communities around ideas.

Just like the public speakers, philosophers, and even gossip-writers of ancient times, today's influencers exercise the power of storytelling and persuasion. Whether it's selling a product, promoting a lifestyle, or rallying support for a social issue, the best influencers create emotional connection first, then trust, and finally action. People follow not only because of what's being shared, but because they feel seen, understood, and inspired. With that pulling in, the audience will feel one with the influencer and defend the cause at all cost. This can turn into online debates within comments with name calling and bullying the other person, all because of a difference in opinion. It's truly another form of bullying. People will go as far as looking up your personal page and trying find more reasons to insult you. Many people have platforms with a focus to discredit other people, online gossip pages, sound familiar?

We've all had moments where we've scrolled through social media, seen a post, and immediately felt offended. Maybe it was a comment about politics, parenting, religion, or even something as simple as someone's opinion about a movie. But here's the thing: being offended isn't always about what was actually said—it's often about how *we interpret* what was said. We assign motives, judgments, and meanings to someone's words or actions. We decide, "They must have meant this" or "They're trying to insult people like me."

This is dangerous because the moment we start assigning motives, we're no longer responding to reality—we're reacting to a story we've written in our own heads. The next step is often sharing the post privately with a friend or within our echo chamber to validate our emotions. You think there's no harm in this, but it's quite the opposite. As you think about the offense and talk about it, your thoughts turn into energy, and that energy eventually turns into action.

That action doesn't have to be directed at the person who made the post. It often spills over into completely unrelated areas of your life:

your workday, your friendships, your family, your relationship with your partner, even how you interact with the barista at your favorite coffee shop. You're carrying that offense with you like emotional luggage, and eventually, it starts leaking out.

A close friend of mine shared a story that perfectly illustrates this. He works remotely and likes to spend time in different coffee shops to get out of the house. One day, while working at a café, he noticed a woman nearby scrolling furiously through social media. Her body language said it all—she was making exasperated sounds, sighing, and shaking her head at the screen. She was clearly upset about something she was reading, most likely politics or current events.

She assumed that everyone around her who looked like her must feel exactly the same way, so she turned to my friend and made a comment, assuming he would agree. In an effort to diffuse her frustration, he gently suggested that perhaps things weren't as bad as they seemed, or that maybe there was more to the story. That single sentence triggered her. She immediately became outraged, raised her voice, and began insulting him — someone she had never met.

All of the energy she had been storing up while scrolling, reading, and reacting finally had an outlet, and unfortunately, my friend was on the receiving end of it. He didn't say another word. He quietly gathered his belongings and left the café.

How did she get to that extreme so quickly? She had spent hours—not days, just hours—reading posts, watching videos, and emotionally connecting with a cause. She trusted the information being presented to her, attached her identity to it, and then reacted. Even though her reaction wasn't healthy, it was still a reaction—an automatic response from a mind primed by constant exposure to outrage.

This is what happens on a neurological level when we get offended on social media. Every time you see something that makes you upset or riled up, your brain releases stress hormones like cortisol and adrenaline. Your fight-or-flight system activates, just like it would if you were being chased by a wild animal. But unlike a real threat, this one doesn't go away. Post after post, comment after comment, your nervous system stays in a low-level state of activation. Over time, this can rewire your brain to expect offense, to look for it, and to live in it.

It also taps into your brain's reward system. The first time you see a post that validates your beliefs, your brain releases dopamine—the feel-good chemical. It feels good to be "right" or to feel part of a group. But then when you see a post that offends you, your brain also lights up— just in a different way. You feel indignation, and that indignation feels powerful. It gives you a surge of energy, and soon you're addicted to scrolling, reacting, and commenting, without realizing you're feeding a cycle that's draining your peace and joy.

Offense isn't just an emotion—it becomes a habit. And habits become lifestyles. When you're constantly offended, your brain becomes more reactive and less reflective. Instead of pausing to think critically or take a breath, you go straight to outrage mode. This can make you more irritable, more anxious, and more likely to see the worst in others—even people who love you. It can even sabotage your health, your career, and your relationships because you're walking around with a short fuse you didn't even know you had.

And this is why social media offense is so powerful—and so dangerous. Because it's subtle. It sneaks up on you one post at a time. Before you know it, you're living in a constant state of irritation, mistrust, and frustration. Your body suffers, your relationships suffer, and your mental health suffers.

Here's the truth: offense is a choice. You may not be able to control what you see online, but you can control how you respond to it. You can decide not to assign motives, not to assume the worst, and not to take the bait. When you do, you're protecting your peace, your health, and your relationships.

In the end, offense on social media is like poison you drink hoping someone else will get sick. It doesn't just hurt the person you're offended at—it hurts *you*. It blocks your ability to heal, to think clearly, to grow, and even to receive constructive feedback from people who genuinely care about you. If you want to live a healthier, happier, more disciplined life, start by protecting your heart online. Don't let a stranger's post have the power to ruin your day—or your life. Your peace is worth more than that.

Family Relationships and Social Media

Let's talk about family relationships and how they affect the way we interact on social media. It's no secret that politics has always had the power to divide people, but in today's digital age, those disagreements often feel amplified. What used to stay at the dinner table is now broadcasted for hundreds—or even thousands—to see with the click of a button. That changes things.

I personally do not recommend debating politics at family gatherings. Most of the time, those conversations end in tension, raised voices, or someone storming off. But now, with the added layer of social media, political disagreements don't just flare up over mashed potatoes—they simmer online for weeks, building frustration before family members even walk through the front door.

I remember a conversation I had last holiday season at the gym. It started with casual small talk: how the kids were doing, how work was going, nothing too deep. As we wrapped up, I asked the woman where she would be spending the holidays. Her entire expression shifted. She said she wasn't sure if she would celebrate Thanksgiving with her parents like usual. When I asked why, she explained that she had grown frustrated with their political posts online. She strongly disagreed with their views, and she wasn't sure if she could sit through a holiday meal without that tension bubbling up.

I paused, listened, and then gently asked, "Outside of politics, how's your relationship with them? Are they good parents and grandparents?"

She stopped for a moment, almost surprised by the question. After reflecting, she said, "Yes, they're great. They love me, and they're wonderful with my kids."

I smiled and offered this thought: "Maybe you could ask ahead of time if politics can be left off the table for one day. Just enjoy being with your parents. Life is too short, and none of us are promised tomorrow. I'd hate for you to miss that time with them and not have the option next year."

We ended the conversation with a smile, and I left her to think about it. I never followed up to see if she visited her parents that Thanksgiving. Months later, when I saw her again, she shared that there had been a passing in her family and that she was heading home for a funeral. My heart sank. I silently hoped she had chosen connection over conflict that previous holiday season.

This moment has stayed with me. It was a reminder of how easy it is to let social media distort the bigger picture of our lives. A disagreement about politics can feel massive when it's constantly on our screens, but when you step back, you realize the core of family isn't built on agreement — it's built on love, shared history, and presence.

Think about it: when the time comes and we look back on our lives, will we really remember who voted for who in a midterm election? Or will we remember the laughter, the meals shared, the traditions that gave us comfort and belonging?

The danger of social media is that it convinces us that our differences are bigger than our relationships. It magnifies small divides until they feel insurmountable. But the truth is, most disagreements don't have to define the entire relationship. Boundaries can help. A simple request like, *"Can we set politics aside this holiday so we can enjoy each other?"* can change everything.

Families, like all relationships, require grace. Grace is the ability to love someone even when you don't agree with them. Grace says, *"I see you for who you are to me, not for the opinions you hold.* When we allow grace to guide us, social media loses its power to fracture our homes.

It's worth asking yourself: is winning the argument worth losing the relationship? For most of us, the answer is no. When a loved one passes away, we don't get the opportunity to revisit those choices. That's why it's so important to protect the connections that matter most while we still can.

I've learned that when it comes to family and social media, sometimes the wisest choice is to log off, mute the posts that upset you, and show up in person with love. The memory of a warm hug will always outlast a heated debate in the comment section.

So, the next time you feel tempted to skip a holiday gathering or distance yourself from family because of what's happening online, pause. Ask yourself the same question I asked that woman at the gym:

"Outside of politics, how's the relationship?" The answer may remind you of what truly matters.

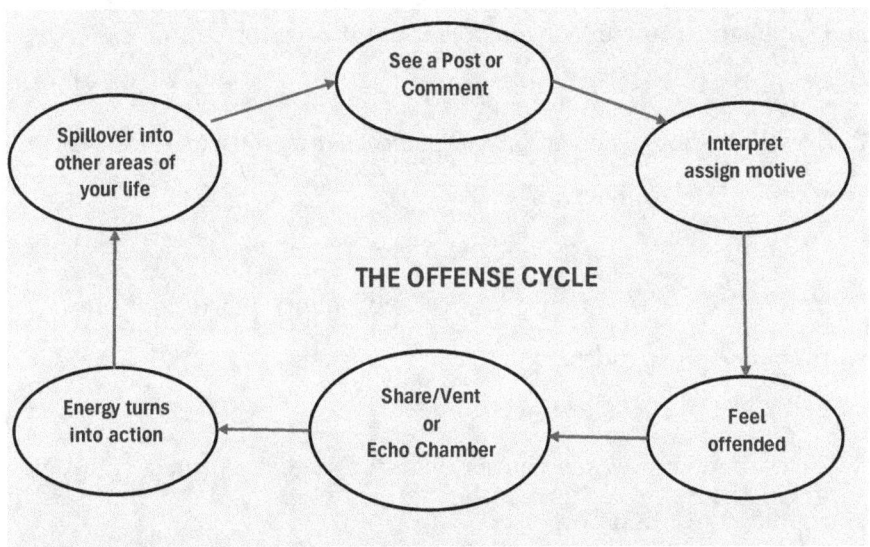

CHAPTER 6 REFLECTION QUESTIONS

1.When was the last time you felt offended by a post on social media, and what story did you tell yourself about the person's motives?

2. How has being inside an online "echo chamber" shaped the way you see those who disagree with you?

3. In what ways has offense you carried online spilled over into your work, family, or friendships?

4. What boundaries could you set on social media to protect your peace and avoid unnecessary offense?

5. Where in your family relationships could you practice more grace instead of letting offense take root?

CHURCH HURT & SPIRITUAL OFFENSE

CHAPTER 7

SPIRITUAL OFFENSE

As I mentioned in the health and wellness chapter, I began to see how people were aborting their lives too soon simply because of the choices they were making around food. I reached a point where it became difficult for me to watch people in church — people with so much spiritual power and authority—while at the same time seeing the physical signs that their health was declining. I could see the vascular fat building on their chest, knowing they were one heartbeat away from cardiac arrest. I noticed the yellow tint in their eyes, a sign that their liver was not functioning at full capacity. I could see the darkness in their skin tones, a visible clue that many were likely diabetic. Over time, it started to look normal to me, as if sickness was simply a part of church culture. And if I'm honest, I began to believe they just didn't care. That thought slowly crept into my spirit: *if they don't care, then why should I?*

It was subtle—like little foxes that slip in unnoticed. At first, I prayed fervently, with warfare prayers, asking God to remove the scales from their eyes, to break the cloud of deception over their minds, to wake them up before it was too late. But as more people brushed aside the urgency of what God was saying through me, I felt the intensity of my prayers lessen. It wasn't intentional. I didn't wake up one morning and decide to stop caring about people's health. The shift was much quieter than that. What I did was begin to conserve my energy for the ones who seemed ready to receive it, the ones who not only listened but also acted on it. At the time, that felt practical. But later, God showed me—it wasn't obedience.

You see, God wasn't asking me to only pour into the willing. He was calling me to intercede for the ones who were still blind, the ones who didn't see the danger of their choices, the ones stuck in a destructive loop of pleasure and endorphins from food. My assignment wasn't about deciding *who deserved prayer*. It was about standing in the gap, regardless of what I could see in the natural.

I only recognized this in hindsight. One day, someone gently asked me if I felt led to pray over the health of the church. My response was quick and casual: "No, thank you." No attitude, no second thought, just as if someone had offered me ketchup and I politely declined. At that moment, I didn't even realize what was happening. But later, as I was talking to the Holy Spirit, He revealed to me that I had taken offense. I stopped in my tracks.

The truth hit me hard: I got offended because I was judging. I had placed my own motives on other people's struggles and assumed they didn't want to change. Because of that assumption, I withdrew my prayers. I was disappointed watching people suffer through health crises, receive God's grace in the form of healing or a second chance, and then go right back to destructive habits. In my mind, it felt like they were slapping God in the face. So, my flesh reasoned, *"If they don't want it, let them deal with the consequences."*

But that's not what God asked of me. That's not the assignment. My role was never to decide who is worthy of intercession.

My role is to intercede *especially* when people don't know what they're doing. I am called to pray on their behalf, ask God for mercy, and plead for repentance. I am called to stand in the gap when they cannot stand for themselves.

Looking back, I see how subtly the enemy worked. The offense came disguised as logic, practicality, and even self-preservation. But in reality, it was pulling me away from the very reason God planted me here: to intercede for those who lack discipline, to cover those who cannot see their own broken patterns, and to lift those who don't yet have the strength to lift themselves.

I now realize that my gift of intercession is not for me, nor is it about pointing out who is right or wrong in my own carnal judgment. It is about identifying what is lacking and standing in prayer until heaven invades that gap. I take full accountability for letting offense cloud my vision, even for a season. I repent for withholding prayers when God called me to pour them out. Today, I recommitted to myself to the assignment—to intercede faithfully, to stay connected to the Vine, and to refuse offense no matter how subtle it comes.

Church Hurt and the Power of Personal Relationship with God

Church people can sometimes be the most manipulative, controlling, and domineering individuals you will ever encounter.

And that's sad— because it is the exact opposite of who God is. I'm referring to the God of Abraham, Isaac, and Jacob, just to be clear.

A very dear friend of mine, Isabella, once shared with me a heartfelt story about her experiences in the church. Her journey is both painful and powerful, and it perfectly illustrates why we cannot afford to confuse *the people of God* with *the character of God.*

The Wound of Legalism

Isabella was in her early 20s when she began attending a very legalistic church. In this place, everything about your outward appearance became a measurement of how "saved" you were. The way you wore your hair, your clothes, lipstick—or even if you painted your nails—were all symbols' people used to judge your level of holiness.

Naturally, this created a toxic environment. Instead of drawing her closer to God, it pushed her deeper into confusion. Isabella loved God and could feel His presence at times within the church, but often, it wasn't God she encountered—it the people. The people made it very difficult for her to feel safe.

Conversations she trusted others with were twisted into gossip. Rumors spread. Criticism followed her everywhere. Ultimately, the spirit of control and judgment drove her away.

The Separation

After leaving that church, Isabella stepped away from church altogether for nearly five years. During that gap, she didn't just avoid attending — she built up a wall in her heart. She would make statements to God like, "I'm not going back," almost as if God Himself and the church building were the same.

But here's the beauty of God: He doesn't stay locked in a building. He pursues us wherever we are. During her time of separation, Isabella experienced something she never expected. She discovered she could have a *personal* relationship with God outside of church walls. She described it as God "wooing her." Whether she was driving in her car, sitting in a club, or hanging out at someone's house—God would whisper gently to her, reminding her of His love. She had intimate conversations with Him, moments where she poured out her heart and felt His presence stronger than she ever had inside a church building.

God was rebuilding her trust. He was showing her that His relationship with her was more important than any institution or religious system. For the first time, she began to see that He was real, that His love was personal, and that His voice was something she could recognize outside of sermons and stained-glass windows.

Relearning Church

Over time, as her trust in God deepened, Isabella began to understand the importance of assembling with other believers again. When she finally stepped into a new church, she was cautious.

This time, though, the environment was different. She found freedom instead of judgment. Acceptance instead of control. Yet, her past experiences made it difficult for her to fully trust. She often pulled back, afraid that history would repeat itself.

This reaction wasn't random — it was neurological. Her past church experiences had carved deep neural pathways in her brain, associating "church" with hurt, betrayal, and manipulation. Every time she walked into a new environment, those old pathways fired, pulling her back into suspicion and fear.

But here's where God's healing power works hand in hand with neuroscience: just as old pathways can be triggered, new pathways can be built. Isabella had to slowly rewire her mind to trust again, creating new associations between church and safety, between people and grace. It took time, but she learned to pause, breathe, and remind herself that *this church was not the old one.*

A Shift in Perspective

Now Isabella lives with a deeper understanding: her relationship with God has nothing to do with a building. It has everything to do with intimacy and private time with the Father.

100

She knows how to maneuver in a place of freedom, discerning the difference between God's presence and man's projections.

She still struggles to fully open up to people, but this isn't from a place of fear anymore, it's wisdom. She understands that people are people. They can be controlling, manipulative, and act out of their own wounds. But that doesn't mean *everyone* is like that. Now, she leans into God's guidance and relies on the discernment of the Spirit to decide who she should draw close to and who she should keep at a distance.

Most importantly, Isabella made a conscious decision: she refuses to live offended by her past. She doesn't allow the old experiences of church hurt to dictate how she engages today. She chose to build trust with God first, and from that foundation, she can re-engage with His people in freedom.

The Lesson in Isabella's Story

Isabella's story is powerful because it reflects what so many people go through. Countless believers walk away from church and never return—not because of God, but because of people. They confuse the failures of humans with the heart of God.

But here's the truth: the church is not God. The people inside a church are not always a reflection of His character. Some are, but others project their wounds, their control, and their dysfunction. That doesn't mean you run away from God. If anything, it means you run closer to Him.

Her journey shows us this: when you root yourself in a personal relationship with God first, you can walk into any church environment with discernment, freedom, and strength. You stop
defining God's character by people and start seeing people through God's character.

That is what breaks the power of offense. That is what frees us to gather again without fear.

CHAPTER 7 REFLECTION QUESTIONS.

1. In what ways have you allowed offense—whether through judgment, disappointment, or frustration with others—to quietly pull you away from your God-given assignments?

2. When you see others struggling with health, habits, or discipline, do you respond with intercession and compassion, or do you withhold prayer because of assumptions about their willingness to change?

3. How have your past experiences with "church hurt" shaped the way you view God, community, and spiritual leadership? Have you ever confused people's flaws with God's character?

4. What old neural pathways or thought patterns might still be shaping your responses when it comes to trust, church environments, or relationships? How can you invite God into the process of renewing and rewiring those pathways?

5. Are you willing to recommit to interceding—even for those who seem blind or resistant—trusting that your role is not to judge who is worthy of prayer, but to stand in the gap as God has called you to?

SELF-OFFENSE & INNER HEALING PERFECTIONISM AND SELF-ABANDONMENT

CHAPTER 8

SELF - OFFENSE

Perfectionism is a never-ending hamster wheel, designed to keep us chasing unrealistic and false expectations. Its pride disguised as wisdom. And it never comes alone — it partners with manipulation, regret, shame, and rebellion.

My close friend Marsha was brave enough to share her story with me about her childhood and her lifelong struggle with self-abandonment. At first, she tied it to things like grades, behavior, and appearance. But as she opened up, she didn't realize that at the root of it all was self-abandonment—and perfectionism was simply the mask she wore to survive.

Her story traces back to a defining moment at age 11. That was the year her parents divorced, and her father walked out of her life. For an 11-year-old girl, that wound cut deep. When a parent leaves, children rarely understand the complexity of adult choices. Instead, they personalize it. *Maybe if I was prettier… If I tried harder in school… If I didn't argue with my brother so much… If I was just good enough, maybe Dad wouldn't have left.*

That belief took root: *If I can be perfect, maybe I won't be abandoned again.*

From that place of rejection, she began searching for love in all the wrong places. Deep down, she felt undeserving, never enough. It became a hamster wheel of constant striving—working out to maintain her body, making sure her hair was always perfect, performing well in school, controlling every external detail—thinking it would somehow guarantee love. But instead of acceptance, she often found more rejection. And with each rejection, the wound of abandonment grew deeper.

Through this cycle, Marsha slowly lost her voice. She learned to silence herself so she wouldn't "rock the boat." She became a people-pleaser, bending herself to gain approval from those she desperately wanted love from. Speaking up felt too risky—what if it pushed someone else away, just like her father? Even now, as an adult, she battles with finding and using her voice. That little 11-year-old inside still fears that standing up for herself will cost her love and bring abandonment all over again.

But here's the turning point: today, Marsha has a relationship with God—a relationship she didn't know she could have at 11. Back then, she didn't have anyone reinforcing her value. No parent telling her she was deeply loved, treasured, and enough. She had only herself. But now, through Christ, she has discovered her identity. She knows nothing she does can separate her from the Father's love.

Still, the old neural pathways run deep. They whisper lies in moments of pressure: *Stay quiet. Don't speak up. Don't risk it. If you're perfect, they won't leave.* That's why she has to be intentional about rewiring her mind. She must stay conscious and choose not to return to the default behavior of the wounded child. She practices opening her mouth, speaking up when she feels dismissed, reminding herself daily: *I am valuable. My voice matters. I am worthy of being heard.*

This is what rewiring the brain looks like. If she doesn't remain aware, the subconscious will pull her right back into the same loop of silence and striving. But when she aligns her thoughts with God's truth, she begins to walk differently. She stops measuring her worth by the approval of others, by comparisons on social media, or by the successes of those around her. Instead, she rests in what God says about her identity.

Here's the deeper truth: self-abandonment isn't just a behavior—it's a way of being. And breaking free requires forgiveness. Forgiveness of the past version of herself who didn't know better. Forgiveness of the choices she made while trying to survive. Forgiveness of the ways she silenced herself or settled for less than she deserved. Without forgiveness, she remains stuck in the past, bound to the little girl at 11 who believed she wasn't enough.

Forgiveness is what untangles her from the hamster wheel. It frees her from regret and rewires her mind for love. Because the truth is—she isn't abandoned. She is seen, chosen, and loved. Faith pulls her forward, teaching her that perfection isn't the goal—healing is. And healing allows her to live in wholeness, without shame, without fear, and without the heavy chains of perfectionism.

Perfectionism will always whisper. But forgiveness—especially forgiveness of self—is what silences the lies and builds a new path forward. That's how the brain is rewired. That's how self-abandonment loses its grip. Being offended at yourself (shame, regret, perfectionism).

Rewiring Your Mind with Forgiveness from Self-Abandonment

Self-abandonment happens when we consistently dismiss our own needs, silence our own voice, or choose people-pleasing over honoring our God-given worth. Over time, this pattern wires the brain to believe:

"My needs don't matter. My voice isn't important. Others deserve more than I do."

That's not just emotional — it's neurological.
Here's how forgiveness and rewiring work together:

Awareness – Catch the Old Wiring

Your brain runs on repeated pathways, like grooves on a record. Self-abandonment creates a "default track" of shame, guilt, or neglect. The first step is noticing when those thoughts show up:

"I don't want to upset them, so I'll stay quiet."

"Their happiness matters more than mine."

This awareness lights up the old neural pathway so you can interrupt it.

Forgiveness – Release the Offense Toward Yourself

Forgiveness isn't just for others. It's about releasing *yourself* from the chains of past choices. When you forgive yourself for abandoning your own needs, you remove the emotional charge that keeps your brain stuck replaying the same story.

You can pray something like:

"Father, I forgive myself for the times I ignored my own needs, silenced my own voice, or betrayed my worth. I release the shame, and I accept Your grace. I choose to walk in truth and love toward myself." This act of self-forgiveness creates a neurological "pattern break."

Rewire – Install New Pathways with Truth + Practice

The brain doesn't erase old pathways; it creates stronger new ones through repetition. After forgiving yourself, you replace self-abandonment thoughts with affirmations grounded in truth:

- *"My needs are valid."*
- *"God has given me worth, and I honor it."*
- *"I can set boundaries and still be loved."*

Each time you choose the new thought over the old, Hebb's Law comes into play: *"Neurons that fire together wire together."* Over time, the new pathway becomes your default.

Embodiment – Align Your Actions with Forgiveness

Forgiveness rewires the heart and mind, but you cement it through action. That means making small daily choices to honor yourself: eating nourishing foods, saying *no* when needed, resting, or speaking up in love. Every aligned action signals safety and respect to your nervous system, reinforcing the new wiring.

Spiritual Integration – Partnering with God's Renewal

Romans 12:2 says, *"Be transformed by the renewing of your mind."* Forgiveness is part of that renewal. When you forgive yourself and walk in truth, you are literally reshaping your brain and aligning it with God's design. You're shifting from self-abandonment to self-honor, from condemnation to grace.

Forgiving yourself for self-abandonment is like taking the power cord out of an old system that ran on shame and plugging it into a new system built on grace and truth. The more you practice, the more your brain rewires to believe, embody, and live from that new reality.

CHAPTER 8 REFLECTION QUESTIONS

1. When you think back to moments in your own life—like Marsha at age 11—what early experiences may have planted the belief that you needed to be "perfect" in order to be loved or accepted?

2. In what ways do you recognize self-abandonment in your daily life? (For example: silencing your voice, putting others' needs above your own, or dismissing your worth.)

3. How does it feel to consider that self-abandonment isn't just emotional, but also neurological—that your brain has been trained to run the "default track" of shame or perfectionism?

4. What would forgiving yourself for self-abandonment look like in your life today? What specific words or prayers would you speak over yourself to release regret and shame?

5. Imagine yourself practicing new thought patterns daily (e.g., "My needs are valid," "I am worthy of love and respect"). What small actions could you take this week to embody those truths and begin rewiring your brain toward self-honor?

Part 3
LIVING
UNOFFENDABLE

CHAPTER 9

The Path to Freedom

Preparing the Heart for Power and Purpose

Freedom is not found in pretending we're unaffected. It's found in finally admitting what has been affecting us—and choosing to heal anyway. Every lesson in this book has been pointing you toward one truth: offense is not just an emotion; it's a trap designed to rewire your brain, distort your perception, and keep you living beneath your divine potential. But when you begin to understand both the spiritual and neurological mechanics of offense, something shifts. You stop reacting and start renewing.

From *Chapter 2* to *Chapter 8*, we've walked through the many disguises' offense wears—the subtle ways it creeps into our relationships, our homes, and even the digital spaces that now shape our daily lives. You've seen how easily your peace can be hijacked by a word, a tone, a post, or a look. But you've also seen that you hold the authority to take that power back.

Let's revisit some of those moments—not to relive them, but to reframe them. Because awareness without reflection doesn't renew the mind; it just gives information without transformation.

When Love Becomes a Battlefield

In Chapter 2, when we explored romantic relationships and dating, we saw that offense often begins when hurt feelings are misinterpreted or personalized. It's not always about what the other person does—it's about how your brain interprets it. When someone says something that stings, your nervous system can immediately activate a "defensive mode." The amygdala—the brain's center for emotional memory and threat detection—lights up, triggering stress hormones like cortisol and adrenaline. Suddenly, your body is on alert, even if no real danger exists.

Spiritually, this mirrors what happens when we allow offense to take root without discernment. Proverbs 18:19 says, *"An offended brother is harder to win back than a fortified city."* Once the brain builds emotional walls, the heart hides behind them. You can't truly receive love when your mind expects rejection or betrayal.

The difference comes when we pause, breathe, and intentionally choose not to react. As I shared in Chapter 2, during my dating experiences, I made it a practice to pause for five seconds whenever someone said something that could sting. Just five seconds—but during that short window, I would ask myself: "Is any part of this story correct? If so, how do I take accountability? If not, what is really driving this comment?" Then I would gently probe the other person with a question, like, "That was an interesting statement—what made you say that?" Most often, people respond based on their past experiences or fears, projecting onto you what they are wrestling with internally. By asking a question instead of reacting immediately, you give their brain—and yours—a chance to slow down. The prefrontal cortex, your reasoning center, starts to engage, calming the amygdala. Your nervous system registers safety, rather than threat.

This small act of curiosity does more than just prevent a misstep—it rewires your brain. Each time you pause instead of reacting, each time you ask questions instead of judging, your mind forms new neural pathways that support patience, discernment, and emotional intelligence. You are teaching yourself how to respond from a place of strength, not fear.

Spiritually, it's the moment your spirit whispers to your flesh: "Peace, be still." Every time you choose to forgive instead of replaying the hurt, your brain literally builds connections of resilience and compassion. This aligns perfectly with God's Word, which says love "keeps no record of wrongs" (1 Corinthians 13:5). Forgiveness here isn't passive; it's active rewiring. It's how offense loses its grip—one intentional pause, one probing question, and one act of love at a time.

By practicing this in my dating life, I learned a profound truth: getting your feelings hurt is inevitable. You cannot always control someone else's words or actions. But offense—harboring resentment, personalizing, and allowing anger to build—is a choice. Choosing to pause, process, and respond with discernment is a way to guard your heart while still being open to love.

Ultimately, this is how we protect ourselves in relationships without building walls that block connection. By separating hurt feelings from offense, you preserve your peace, strengthen your heart, and open the door to God's love flowing through you. Over time, your brain learns to anticipate safety rather than threat, and your spirit grows stronger, anchored in grace rather than fear.

Family Triggers and Emotional Echoes

In *Chapter 3*, we explored the hidden pain that shapes how we respond to offense—pain that often starts long before we realize it. I shared how my own story began with loss at just four years old when my mother passed away and how that single moment shaped the wiring of my brain. Losing a parent at such a young age imprints confusion, fear, and a desperate search for security. When my father remarried; that search became a cycle of trying to earn love that should have been freely given. Verbal and physical abuse during those years taught my nervous system to live on high alert—to see danger even when there wasn't any. I didn't know it then, but my amygdala was firing constantly, and my prefrontal cortex, the part that helps regulate emotions and reason, was struggling to keep up.

That's how offense begins—not just through events, but through **the brain's learned response** to pain. When someone who is supposed to love you becomes the source of harm, your brain learns to equate love with danger.

Forgiveness, in that context, feels like betrayal of the self. That's why it can take decades to unlearn survival wiring.

But God doesn't waste pain. He rewires what the world has broken. Years later, I stood at my father's funeral face-to-face with the woman who had been a source of so much hurt. For years, I imagined how I'd react if I ever saw her again. Would I freeze? Would anger take over? Would I revert back to the little girl who just wanted to be seen and loved? None of that happened. Because by the time I stood in front of her, my brain—and my heart—had been renewed.

What neuroscience would call *emotional regulation* was, for me, the evidence of grace. My nervous system was calm. I was not "triggered." I walked up to her, hugged her, and gave my condolences. It wasn't a performance — it was peace. The peace that comes from doing the hard work of forgiveness long before the moment demands it. My heart had already rehearsed love; my mind had already rehearsed grace.

That's the secret neuroscience never tells you: your brain can be trained for peace the same way it's been trained for pain. The more you practice forgiveness, compassion, and curiosity, the stronger those neural pathways become. Over time, your brain stops defaulting to fear and starts defaulting to faith.

Spiritually, that's what renewing your mind looks like. It's not ignoring your past—it's reinterpreting it. I didn't walk into that funeral as a broken child, I walked in as a healed woman. And when I walked out, I carried only love for my father and gratitude for the growth that pain had produced. That is freedom. That is the fruit of refusing to take the bait.

The Digital Battlefield

And then came *Chapter 6*—social media and public spaces. This chapter was about the battlefield you carry in your pocket. In a world designed for outrage, peace becomes an act of rebellion. Every scroll, every video, every comment has the potential to activate your amygdala. The more emotionally charged the post, the more your brain releases cortisol, adrenaline, and dopamine—creating a chemical cocktail of stress and reward. It's why people can feel exhausted after being online for ten minutes, even if they never left their couch.

The story of the woman in the café reminded us how easily offense spills into real life. She wasn't just mad at a stranger online; she was neurologically wired to stay in fight mode. What she consumed shaped what she became.

Scripture echoes this: *"As a man thinketh in his heart, so is he."* What you meditate on shapes not only your thoughts but your brain's literal structure. That's why Paul's command in Philippians 4:8 is both spiritual and scientific — *"Whatever is true, whatever is noble, whatever is right...think on these things."* He was giving us a neurological key to peace.

When you fast from outrage, mute the noise, and train your attention toward gratitude and grace, your brain releases serotonin instead of cortisol. Your body calms. Your perspective clears. You start to feel more like yourself again — the version that was never meant to live in reaction, but in reflection.

Practical Neuroscience + Biblical Tools to Stop Taking the Bait

So how do we stay free? How do we live in the world without letting the world live inside us?

First, awareness. When you notice that rise in your chest, that tightening in your throat, **pause**. Don't justify it — observe it. You're not weak for feeling it; you're wise for catching it. That's your amygdala signaling "threat." But here's your power: you get to decide if it's real or rehearsed. Take a deep breath. The moment you breathe intentionally, you re-engage the prefrontal cortex—the seat of logic, discernment, and faith.

Second, confession. Scripture tells us to "take every thought captive." That's not metaphorical — it's neurological. When you name what you're feeling, the brain's limbic system begins to calm. Naming neutralizes. It's why saying, "I feel disappointed" often brings more peace than suppressing it.

Third, redirection. This is the renewing of the mind. When the thought comes—

"They don't respect me," "I'll never be enough," "I can't trust them"—don't argue with it. **Replace it. Speak the Word**.
"I am loved. I am secure. I have the mind of Christ." Each declaration builds new neural associations that align your biology with your belief.

You're not just practicing self-control—you're practicing spiritual authority.

Renewing the Mind Exercises

1. **Breathwork for Renewal:**

   When you feel triggered, close your eyes and inhale for four counts, exhale for six. As you breathe, repeat: **"Peace be still."** The slower exhale activates the vagus nerve, signaling safety to your entire nervous system. Spiritually, it's a reminder that you live under grace, not chaos.

2. **The 5-Minute Reframe:**

   Journal about the offense. Write what happened, how it made you feel, and what story your mind created. Then, ask: **"Is this truth, or is this trauma speaking?"** Choose to write one sentence that reflects what God says about you instead. That new sentence becomes your anchor.

3. **Gratitude Replacement:**

   When your mind starts replaying the moment of offense, **list three things you're grateful** for instead. Gratitude doesn't erase pain, but it shifts the brain's attention to abundance, activating pathways of hope instead of fear.

These practices are not "self-help"—they're *soul alignment*. They bring your biology into agreement with your belief.

Strengthening Your Unoffendable Muscle

Just like physical muscles, your ability to stay unoffended strengthens with repetition. The first time you pause instead of reacting, it feels awkward. The second time, it feels intentional. The tenth time, it feels natural. Eventually, peace becomes your default response.

Think of your "unoffendable muscle" as spiritual endurance training. Every act of forgiveness builds neural and spiritual resilience. Every boundary rooted in love builds emotional integrity. Every time you choose presence over pride, your heart becomes stronger.

This is what Paul meant in Galatians 5:22–23 when he listed the fruit of the Spirit: love, joy, peace, patience, kindness, goodness, faithfulness, gentleness, and self-control. These aren't personality traits—they're neural outcomes of spiritual discipline. The more you practice them, the more your brain mirrors heaven.

Living in Freedom

You've now seen that freedom isn't an event — it's a lifestyle. It's choosing reflection over reaction, awareness over accusation, peace over pride.

The enemy's greatest strategy has always been distraction, keeping your focus on who offended you instead of who called you. But your focus determines your frequency. The moment you fix your mind on what's true, your brain aligns with it. You literally shift your internal state from chaos to coherence.

You've practiced this through the love wounds of Chapter 2, the family mirrors of Chapter 3, and the digital storms of Chapter 6. You've seen how offense hides in plain sight—and how awareness exposes it. Now, it's time to move beyond awareness into alignment. **Pause. Breathe. Reflect.** You've seen the patterns. Now prepare your heart. The next chapter isn't about surviving offense—it's about walking in the strength that comes after. When your mind is renewed, your peace is restored. And when your peace is restored, your purpose becomes clear.

In Chapter 10: Walking in Power & Purpose, we'll step into what comes next—how to live from this renewed space, how to discern without judging, how to lead without reacting, and how to carry peace like a mantle in every environment you enter.

You are no longer defined by what hurts you. You are shaped by what heals you. And that healing begins and ends in renewal.
You've done the inner work. Now it's time to walk in it.

CHAPTER 9 REFLECTION QUESTIONS

1. When you think back on your romantic or relational experiences, what patterns of offense have you noticed repeating — and how might those be signals of unhealed emotional memories rather than current reality?

2. In your family dynamics, where do you still feel emotionally "hooked"? What new perspective can you choose that aligns with renewal rather than reaction?

3. How has social media subtly shaped your beliefs, emotions, or sense of peace? What boundaries or new habits can help you protect your mental and spiritual focus?

4. Which daily practice from this chapter's tools could help you strengthen your "unoffendable muscle" — journaling, breathwork, prayer, or pausing before reacting?

5. As you prepare to step into *Chapter 10: Walking in Power & Purpose*, what truth do you now believe about yourself that you didn't when you started this book?

WALKING IN POWER & PURPOSE

CHAPTER 10

HOW FORGIVENESS FREES YOUR FUTURE

I have been teaching on the power of forgiveness since 2016, and one thing I always emphasize is that forgiveness is not an abstract concept, it is a **lived experience**, a discipline you cultivate within yourself. I teach from a place of authenticity, meaning I teach from where I have personally walked, stumbled, and learned to master the tools necessary to maintain the discipline of living in forgiveness. I have learned that forgiveness is not a one-time event; it is a daily, conscious choice. It is choosing to refuse the bait of offense and letting God's love rewrite your story instead of letting past pain dictate your future.

In my second book, *The Power of the 'F' Word in the Workplace*, I explore a principle I call **"looking at the innocence."** The idea is simple yet transformative: if the person who hurt you truly understood the impact of their behavior, would they still have done it? In my experience, nine times out of ten, the answer is no. Most people do not act from a place of malice; they act from their own pain, their own unhealed wounds, their own limited understanding. I know this firsthand because I have done things that unknowingly hurt others, completely oblivious to the effect of my actions. Recognizing this truth transforms how we respond to offense. It allows us to step back, see the intention—or lack thereof—and choose a response that aligns with love, integrity, and purpose rather than reactivity.

Understanding this principle has radically altered how I show up in my relationships, at work, and in life. I have come to realize that I can never control anyone else's behavior, but I have full authority over how I respond. This is where true power resides. I no longer operate from a place of offense or defensiveness because I refuse to let someone else's actions dictate my peace or my trajectory. Instead, I strive to function from a state of **conscious awareness**, observing the moment without becoming entangled in it. I watch the intent behind actions, separate it from the effect, and choose a response that strengthens my integrity and preserves my peace.

This is not to say that living in forgiveness is always easy. Forgiveness requires discipline—a **daily, intentional commitment to let go of the past**, to reject the narrative that keeps us small, and to embrace the freedom that comes from aligning with God's truth. The brain naturally resists this because it wants to survive by holding onto offenses. Neuroscience shows us that when we ruminate on past hurt, the amygdala—the fear center of the brain—activates as if we are in immediate danger. Cortisol floods the system, triggering stress, defensiveness, and, over time, even physical illness. Choosing forgiveness is literally rewiring your brain, teaching it that safety, love, and peace are stronger than fear, resentment, or anger. Every time you forgive, you strengthen the prefrontal cortex, the area of the brain responsible for decision-making, empathy, and emotional regulation. You are literally building new neural pathways of resilience, compassion, and freedom.

Spiritually, this aligns perfectly with the biblical principle of letting go. Jesus said in Matthew 6:14–15, *"For if you forgive others their trespasses, your heavenly Father will also forgive you, but if you do not forgive others their trespasses, neither will your Father forgive your trespasses."* Forgiveness is not just a moral instruction—it is medicine for the soul. Every time we release bitterness, every time we refuse to rehearse the hurt, we are participating in our own spiritual and neurological transformation. We are reclaiming the authority God has given us over our hearts and minds, choosing to walk in power instead of being chained by offense.

I know firsthand how forgiveness transforms life. My own journey has been marked by experiences that could have left me bitter, resentful, or closed off. I have experienced loss, betrayal, misunderstanding, and rejection—sometimes in ways that cut deeply. Yet, each painful experience became an opportunity to practice forgiveness and see beyond the surface behavior of others. I chose to forgive—not for them, but for me. I chose to release the past so I could fully step into my present and future without carrying the weight of what had happened.

Forgiveness also intersects with **self-forgiveness**, which is often overlooked. How many of us allow our own mistakes, regrets, and failures to keep us trapped in a cycle of shame or self-condemnation? I have learned that you cannot truly walk in purpose if you're still punishing yourself for past decisions. The same principle applies "look at the innocence." You did what you could with what you knew at the time. You acted from your level of understanding and maturity. To forgive yourself is to release your mind from the prison of "what if" and "if only." It is to recognize that every experience—positive or negative—has been a building block, shaping you into the woman or man God created you to be.

One of the most powerful aspects of forgiveness is its ability to **free your future**. When you carry offense, it clouds your perception and limits your potential. It keeps you looking backward, relieving pain that has no productive place in the present. But when you forgive, you step out of the past and open yourself to the possibilities God has prepared for you. Philippians 3:13–14 reminds us: *"Brothers and sisters, I do not consider myself yet to have taken hold of it. But one thing I do: Forgetting what is behind and straining toward what is ahead, I press on toward the goal to win the prize for which God has called me heavenward in Christ Jesus."* Forgiveness allows us to forget—not in the sense of erasing memory, but in the sense of **releasing the emotional grip** that past experiences have over our lives. It is a conscious decision to strain toward purpose rather than be entangled in pain.

Neuroscience also underscores this truth. Research shows that people who consistently practice forgiveness experience **lower blood**

pressure, reduced stress hormones, improved immune function, and increased emotional resilience. Their brains are literally less reactive to perceived threats because the neural circuitry of threat and defense has been rebalanced by repeated acts of compassion and release. In other words, forgiveness is both **spiritual obedience and physical wellness.** Choosing forgiveness is literally choosing life—life that is abundant, empowered, and aligned with God's purpose.

Forgiveness also allows us to see **divine orchestration** in our lives. When I reflect on my own past, I see how every painful experience, every offense, and every misunderstanding was shaping me for a greater purpose. Had I not walked through broken relationships, personal loss, or professional setbacks, I would not have the depth of empathy, wisdom, and strength I now bring to others. Forgiveness is the lens through which we see God's hand guiding us even when circumstances feel chaotic. It is the tool that allows us to move from victimhood to victory, from pain to purpose, and from reaction to intentional response.

I often teach people to **practice forgiveness in incremental steps**, especially when the offense is deep or ongoing. You don't have to feel "ready" to forgive; you just have to "make a decision" to start. Begin by recognizing the innocence or limited understanding of the other person. Then, release the emotional charge by consciously refusing to rehearse the hurt. Finally, replace resentment with a

proactive choice: what positive action can I take that aligns with God's purpose? Over time, these steps compound, transforming the neural pathways of bitterness into pathways of love, compassion, and empowerment.

Forgiveness is also about **maintaining your focus on your target,** your purpose, and your God-given destiny. I have learned that when I dwell on what others say or do to me, I am distracted from my mission. I am called to a higher purpose, and offense is a thief of both peace and progress. By refusing to take the bait, I preserve my energy, focus, and creativity for what truly matters: living a life anchored in God, aligned with my values, and pursuing the calling placed upon me.

I have witnessed this principle play out in both personal and professional settings. People often ask me, *"How do you remain calm when someone does something deliberately hurtful?"* My answer is simple: I recognize that their behavior says more about them than it does about me. I separate the person from the pain they cause, and I allow God to be the judge. My responsibility is to maintain my integrity, my peace, and my focus on purpose. I refuse to give anyone else power over my future by holding onto offense.

There is also a liberating sense of **joy and freedom** that comes from walking in forgiveness. When you let go of the burden of resentment, you open yourself to authentic relationships, clearer decision-making, and a sense of inner peace that cannot be shaken by external circumstances. You are no longer a hostage to past pain, but an active participant in your own destiny.

Ephesians 4:31–32 reminds us: *"Get rid of all bitterness, rage and anger, brawling and slander, along with every form of malice. Be kind and compassionate to one another, forgiving each other, just as in Christ God forgave you."* Walking in forgiveness is walking in alignment with God's design for your life.

Finally, forgiveness is **forward-looking**. It does not condone wrongdoing, but it releases you from being tethered to it. It transforms the "story" of your past into a narrative of strength and growth. It allows you to walk boldly into your calling, confident that your past mistakes, your pain, and even the betrayals you have endured cannot define you. They are steppingstones, each one a lesson, each one an opportunity to cultivate resilience, wisdom, and a heart that mirrors God's own.

I challenge you today to embrace forgiveness not as an abstract ideal but as a daily discipline. Practice it in the small moments and in the big ones. Look for the innocence behind actions, release the emotional grip of offense, and intentionally align your response with love, wisdom, and purpose. In doing so, you will not only experience the peace of God but also the tangible transformation of your mind, heart, and body.

Walking in forgiveness is walking in power. It is walking in purpose. And most importantly, it is walking free. The future is no longer a shadow of past pain—it is a canvas waiting for the masterpiece God has designed uniquely for you.

Maintaining an Unoffendable Heart in All Areas of Life

If there is one thing I've learned on my journey of spiritual and emotional growth, it's that peace is not the absence of conflict — it's the mastery of response. To live with an *unoffendable heart* is to live from a place of deep spiritual maturity, emotional regulation, and unwavering trust in God. It is to say, "No matter what happens, I will not give my peace away."

The truth is that offense is one of the most subtle traps the enemy uses to derail our purpose. It doesn't always come as a big betrayal or public humiliation. Sometimes it shows up quietly — through a comment, a misunderstanding, a lack of recognition, or unmet expectations. It sneaks in when someone forgets to call back, when a coworker gets credit for your effort, or when a loved one's tone feels dismissive. Offense is sneaky because it hides under the illusion of *justified emotion.* It whispers, "You have the right to be angry," and before you know it, you've taken the bait.

But here's the danger: once offense enters the heart, it starts to contaminate perception. The mind begins to replay the event, attaching stories and emotions to it. The Reticular Activating System (RAS) that powerful filter in your brain — begins scanning for evidence to support the feeling of injustice. It keeps you in a loop of proof-gathering, making sure every new interaction confirms the old wound. Without realizing it, your brain becomes wired for defensiveness, resentment, and emotional vigilance.

Spiritually speaking, this is why Proverbs 4:23 warns us, *"Above all else, guard your heart, for everything you do flows from it."* To guard your heart means to protect your inner environment from becoming polluted by offense, bitterness, or resentment. When you maintain an unoffendable heart, you choose to live free from emotional manipulation. You are declaring that nothing and no one outside of you will determine the condition of your inner world.

The Science of Staying Unoffended

From a neuroscience perspective, every time you choose not to take offense, you are actually retraining your brain's default response to perceived threats. The amygdala — your brain's alarm system — wants to interpret emotional discomfort as danger. It activates the fight-or-flight response, flooding your system with cortisol and adrenaline. But when you consciously choose calmness, compassion, or curiosity instead of reacting, you engage your prefrontal cortex — the part of your brain responsible for higher reasoning, empathy, and emotional regulation.

This repeated act of choosing peace over offense builds new neural pathways that support emotional resilience. Over time, your brain learns that you are safe even when others behave poorly. You no longer need to defend your identity or dignity because your sense of worth isn't dependent on external validation — it's anchored in God's truth.

Romans 12:2 reminds us, *"Do not be conformed to the pattern of this world, but be transformed by the renewing of your mind."* Every time you refuse to take offense, you are literally renewing your mind — interrupting old patterns of emotional reactivity and replacing them with patterns of grace and strength.

Understanding the Root of Offense

At the root of offense is unmet expectation. We expect people to act, speak, or respond in a certain way, and when they don't, disappointment arises. But disappointment left unaddressed turns into offense. And offense, if nurtured, turns into bitterness. This emotional progression is like a spiritual infection — it starts small but can spread quickly if left untreated.

One of the most transformative truths I've learned is this: *people cannot give what they do not have.* Expecting emotional maturity, empathy, or spiritual awareness from someone who has not yet developed those capacities is setting yourself up for disappointment. When I began to truly internalize this, it changed everything. I stopped expecting people to understand me at a depth they hadn't yet reached within themselves. Instead, I began to view every offense as an opportunity to practice compassion and strengthen my emotional and spiritual maturity.

An unoffendable heart doesn't mean you become numb or detached — it means you become *anchored*. You still feel emotions, but you process them through understanding and grace rather than reaction. You acknowledge pain, but you don't allow it to control your narrative.

The Biblical Model of an Unoffendable Heart

Jesus modeled this perfectly. Imagine being betrayed by one of your disciples, denied by another, and abandoned by the rest — all while knowing you were innocent. Yet, even on the cross, He said,

"Father, forgive them, for they know not what they do." (Luke 23:34). That statement is the ultimate demonstration of an unoffendable heart.

Jesus saw the **innocence in their ignorance**. He understood that they were acting from blindness, not intentional cruelty. That's the same mindset we must cultivate if we are to walk in true power and purpose. To maintain an unoffendable heart, you must train yourself to look beyond the action and discern the condition of the soul behind it.

When you understand this, you begin to live from love instead of reaction. You realize that the person who hurt you is also hurting. The colleague who disrespected you might be insecure. The friend who betrayed your trust might be projecting their own fear of abandonment. When you start to see through the lens of compassion, offense loses its grip.

Practical Tools for Guarding Your Heart

1. **Pause Before You React.**

   The moment you feel the rise of irritation or hurt, pause. Take a deep breath and engage your prefrontal cortex. Ask yourself, *"What's really happening here?"* Often, the initial offense is not about the moment itself but about a deeper trigger — something that touches an old wound or belief. When you pause, you give your brain time to reset and your spirit time to listen.

2. **Ask God for Perspective.**

   Pray, "Lord, show me what I need to see here." God's wisdom always reveals what human perception cannot. He might show you that the situation is a mirror, reflecting something in you that still needs healing. Or He might show you that this moment is a test — a chance to practice spiritual discipline and demonstrate grace under pressure.

3. **Release the Need to Be Right.**

   Offense thrives on ego. It wants to prove, defend, and justify. But peace lives in surrender. When you let go of the need to be right, you open the door for reconciliation, growth, and healing. Remember, you can win the argument and still lose your peace.

4. **Shift from Reaction to Response.**

   A reaction is automatic; a response is intentional. Reactions come from emotion; responses come from awareness. Respond from your values, not your wounds. This is how you maintain authority over your mind and emotions.

5. **Bless Instead of Curse.**

   This is one of the most spiritually powerful tools you can use. When someone offends you, speak a blessing over them. Romans 12:14 says, *"Bless those who persecute you; bless and do not curse."* It's impossible to stay bitter toward someone you continually bless. Blessing interrupts the cycle of bitterness and rewires your emotional state toward peace.

Applying It in Every Area of Life

1. **In Relationships:**

   Maintaining an unoffendable heart in relationships means choosing to love over ego. When conflict arises, remind yourself that you and the other person are not opponents — you are both humans learning, growing, and sometimes failing forward.

Reply with curiosity, not accusation. Instead of saying, "How could you say that to me?" try, "Help me understand what you meant." That one shift can disarm tension and invite healing.

2. In the Workplace:

Offense in the workplace is one of the biggest distractions to productivity and leadership growth. Whether it's a boss overlooking your contribution or a coworker taking credit for your work, offense can quietly drain your motivation. But when you lead with an unoffendable heart, you stand out as a person of stability and integrity. You become someone people trust because you're not easily shaken. Remember: leadership isn't about controlling others — it's about controlling your response.

3. In Family:

Family offense cuts the deepest because it's tied to belonging and identity. When offense arises at home, remember that forgiveness does not mean approval — it means release. It means you refuse to let generational patterns of pain dictate your behavior. When you forgive family, you not only heal yourself, you disrupt generational cycles and open the door for new patterns of grace.

4. In Ministry or Leadership:

Offense in ministry can be the most spiritually damaging because it often comes wrapped in righteous language. But remember — the higher your calling, the more intentional your discipline must be. When people criticize, misunderstand, or misjudge you, let it refine you, not define you. God will always vindicate His servants. Your job is to keep your heart pure so your gift can flow freely.

The Reward of an Unoffendable Heart

When you live unoffended, you live untouchable. It doesn't mean you're invincible to hurt — it means hurt no longer has authority over your peace. You move through life lighter, freer, and more in tune with God's voice because there's no clutter in your heart to muffle it.

An unoffendable heart is a healed heart. It's one that has learned to see beyond the surface, to recognize that everyone is fighting unseen battles, and to choose empathy over ego. It is a heart that has surrendered its right to be angry in exchange for the privilege of peace.

The beauty of this way of living is that it magnifies your power. Offense is bondage; forgiveness is freedom. Every time you choose to remain unoffended, you take back authority over your mind, emotions, and destiny. You become unstoppable — not because life gets easier, but because you are no longer controlled by it.

So, make it your daily goal: *I will maintain an unoffendable heart.* Not because everyone deserves it, but because your peace and your purpose are too valuable to risk.

When your heart is unoffendable, your spirit stays unshaken — and that, my friend, is what it truly means to walk in power and purpose.

CHAPTER 10 REFLECTION QUESTIONS

1. **What past offense or memory still tries to claim space in your mind and heart—and how is it subtly shaping your choices today?**

   Take a moment to reflect on whether your reactions, relationships, or thought patterns are being influenced by an old wound. What might change in your life if you released that pain and allowed forgiveness to rewrite that part of your story?

2. **How can you begin to "look at the innocence" in the people who have hurt you?**

   Think of a specific situation or person who has caused offense. If you considered that they acted from their own pain or limited understanding, how would that shift your emotional response? What new level of empathy or peace could emerge from that perspective?

3. **Where are you still trying to control others instead of mastering your own response?**

   True power comes from self-governance, not control. Reflect on one area of life—family, relationships, work, or ministry— where offense or disappointment has taken your focus off your purpose. What would it look like to take your power back through conscious awareness and emotional discipline?

4. **What does an "unoffendable heart" look like for you right now?**

Describe what it would mean to live each day with a calm, anchored heart that refuses to give away peace. How would your conversations, decisions, and relationships change if you consistently paused, prayed, and responded instead of reacted?

5. **How has forgiveness expanded your capacity for purpose, love, and leadership?**

Reflect on a time when choosing forgiveness brought unexpected clarity, strength, or opportunity. How did releasing that weight open new doors or align you more deeply with your God-given destiny? What is God asking you to release next so you can step fully into your power and purpose?

BONUS CHAPTER

The Death That Brings Freedom
Dying to Self So the Spirit Can Lead

A dead person can't get offended.

That's something I have to remind myself daily.

Paul said in *1 Corinthians 15:31*, "I die daily." He wasn't speaking poetically — he was describing a spiritual discipline. Dying to the flesh is not a one-time act; it's a daily surrender. It is the process of letting go of our own desires, reactions, and ego so that our spirit can fully lead. When we live from the flesh, offense becomes easy — because the flesh always wants to be right, to be heard, to be validated. But when the flesh is crucified, offense has nowhere to live.

All sin — and every form of offense — comes from three areas: **the pride of life, the lust of the eyes, and the lust of the flesh** (*1 John 2:16*). These are the root systems of our carnal nature. Pride says, "I deserve better." Lust says, "I need this to be satisfied." And the flesh says, "I want what feels good now." Each of these is a voice that pulls us away from peace and pushes us into confusion. When the flesh leads, offense thrives, because our sense of identity becomes rooted in how others treat us instead of who God says we are.

To live a Spirit-led life, you must make a conscious decision to die to the flesh every single day. This means choosing humility over pride, obedience over comfort, and spiritual clarity over emotional chaos. Dying to self is not a loss — it is the greatest gain. It is the trade-off that allows you to walk in constant communion with God, free from the noise of ego, insecurity, and emotional reaction.

Think of it this way: fasting is a physical representation of killing the flesh. When you fast, you deny the body's cravings to strengthen your spirit's sensitivity. You are quieting the world's noise so you can hear the whisper of the Father. God is always speaking — but if your spirit is clogged with worldly distractions, His voice will sound faint and distorted.

Imagine a water pipe running from miles away, meant to bring you clean, refreshing water. If that pipe is filled with dirt, trash, or debris, the water can't flow freely. By the time it reaches you, it's contaminated — it doesn't taste the same. That's exactly what happens when we allow our minds and hearts to become cluttered with offense, pride, and worldly thinking. The flow of the Spirit is still moving toward us, but we can't receive it clearly because our spiritual pipeline is blocked.

The daily death to the flesh is what clears that pipeline. It's what keeps your spiritual hearing sharp and your heart pure. When you die to yourself, you are not losing power — you are reclaiming it. You are positioning yourself to receive directly from God without interference.

Living an unoffendable life is not about ignoring pain or pretending you're not hurt — it's about being so anchored in the Spirit that the actions of others cannot pull you out of alignment with peace. The flesh reacts; the Spirit responds. The flesh holds grudges, the Spirit releases. The flesh wants control, the Spirit trusts God.

Jesus modeled this perfectly. He died not only for us but as an example *to* us. His death represents the ultimate surrender — the full yielding of the flesh so the Spirit could bring new life. When He said, "It is finished," it wasn't just about salvation — it was a declaration that the power of the flesh no longer ruled. Through His death, we gained access to true life.

Every day you choose to die to your flesh, you are participating in that same resurrection power. You are saying, "Not my will, but Yours be done." You are choosing Spirit over self, peace over pride, and purpose over offense.

If you truly want to walk in power and purpose, you must die to yourself daily. Because the truth is, a dead person can't be offended — and a surrendered person can't be shaken.

So, make this your declaration:

"Today, I die to me — so Christ can fully live through me."

When you live from that place, you'll find that peace isn't something you chase; it becomes who you are.

Appendix

Bible Verse Reference Table of Contents

This guide lists every Scripture included in *Don't Take the Bait*, organized by chapter. Each verse connects biblical truth with the neuroscience of forgiveness, emotional healing, and the renewing of the mind.

---

1 Corinthians 6:19–20 – Your body is God's temple; caring for it is spiritual obedience.

Chapter 6 – Social Media & Public Spaces

Philippians 4:8 – Think on what is true, noble, right, and pure; protect your mental diet.

Chapter 7 – Church Hurt

James 1:19–20 – Be quick to listen, slow to speak, slow to anger.

Matthew 18:15–17 – Address conflict in love; seek restoration, not retaliation.

Chapter 8 – Self-Offense & Inner Healing

Romans 12:2 – Renew your mind daily, releasing shame and rewiring for truth.

Psalm 139:14 – You are fearfully and wonderfully made; your worth is not determined by mistakes.

Chapter 9 – The Path to Freedom

Proverbs 18:19 – Revisit your emotional walls; let grace rebuild connection.

2 Corinthians 10:5 – Take every thought captive; train your mind to obey Christ.

John 8:36 – Whom the Son sets free is free indeed.

Chapter 10 – Walking in Power & Purpose

Philippians 3:13–14 – Forget what is behind and press forward toward your purpose.

Galatians 2:20 – Die to self so that Christ may live through you.

Bonus Chapter – Dying to the Flesh Daily

1 Corinthians 15:31 – I die daily; kill the flesh so the spirit may lead.

1 John 2:16 – The lust of the flesh, eyes, and pride of life come from the world, not from God.

Luke 23:34 – Father, forgive them; the ultimate picture of an unoffendable heart.

ACKNOWLEDGMENTS

Writing this book has been a transformative journey within itself. Reflecting on the lessons of my past—how I responded to pain, disappointment, and heartbreak—reminded me that truly, nothing in life is in vain. Every experience, whether joyful or difficult, served a divine purpose. Without the heartaches, the letdowns, and the seasons of disappointment, this message would not exist.

First and foremost, I give all glory and praise to my Lord and Savior, Jesus Christ. It is because of His resurrection power that I am able to walk in forgiveness and now share that power with others. His grace continues to guide my every word and every step.

To all the people who entrusted me with your stories—thank you. I pray that you were blessed in sharing and that my translation of your experiences honors your truth. I don't take your trust for granted; your vulnerability has helped bring this message to life, and I am deeply grateful.

To my best friend, **Micheala** — thank you for always being honest with me, for your unwavering support, and for believing in my dreams even when I questioned them. I love you more than you know.

To my sister, **Karim** — thank you for taking the time to read my book and for writing the beautiful foreword. Your passion for success and for helping others inspires me every day. I love your drive, your wisdom, and the example you set.

To my amazing friend, **Ken** — thank you for holding me accountable throughout this process and helping my vision come alive. Your encouragement and belief in this project kept me focused and faithful. I will forever be grateful for your friendship.

To all my **collaborators and business partners**, your support, creativity, and contribution made this book possible. You helped shape an idea into something extraordinary, and I couldn't have done it without you.

To my church family at **Reach City**, and to **Pastors Isiah and Kelli Williams**, thank you for your prayers, your covering, and for always seeing the gifts God placed within me. Thank you for allowing me to borrow your parents as my own—they have been a true blessing to my spirit and my journey.

To my beautiful **Godmothers, Angie and Pam** — thank you for your prayers, your love, and for feeling me in the Spirit during the moments I couldn't find the strength to pray for myself. My life is forever changed because of your presence, faith, and guidance.

Finally, to every reader who holds this book in your hands — my prayer is that you understand that everything begins in the mind. Taking the bait of offense is always a choice. God has already given you dominion over your thoughts, your emotions, and your life. My hope is that you choose freedom, peace, and the unshakable joy that comes from walking in forgiveness.

With love and gratitude,

Amanda V. Hill

About the Author

Amanda V. Hill is an author, certified neuroscience coach, corporate leader, and devoted mother who is passionate about helping people break free from mental, emotional, and spiritual bondage. With a unique ability to blend biblical truth with neuroscience, Amanda teaches practical tools that renew the mind, restore peace, and empower people to live in alignment with God's purpose for their lives.

Amanda is the author of *The Faith Within Me, The Power of the "F" Word in the Workplace,* and *Your Roadmap to Success: 5 Strategies for Goal Attainment.* Each of her books carries a consistent theme— transformation begins in the mind. She believes that by understanding how God designed the brain and applying His Word intentionally, anyone can experience true freedom and lasting change.

In her professional career, Amanda serves in a senior-level corporate role, where she has led leadership and operations and account management across national teams. Outside the corporate world, she has been an influential voice in the fitness industry since 2006, teaching both the discipline of the body and the renewal of the mind.

Amanda is deeply connected to her local church and community, where she continues to mentor, teach, and lead others toward spiritual growth and healing. As a mother of four, she understands the delicate balance between faith, family, and purpose—and brings that wisdom into her work, her writing, and her ministry.

Her mission is simple yet powerful: to help people rewire their minds with the Word of God, walk in forgiveness, and live free from the traps that hold them back.

To learn more about Amanda's books, coaching, and speaking engagements, visit:

🌐 www.amandavhill.com

📱 Follow her on social media: @AmandaVHill

KEYSTOBALANCE PUBLISHING

EVERYONE HAS A STORY.

WE HELP YOU UNCOVER IT!

SHAPE IT!

AND SHARE IT WITH THE WORLD.

WWW.KEYSTOBALANCE.NET

www.ingramcontent.com/pod-product-compliance
Lightning Source LLC
Chambersburg PA
CBHW060428130626
46555CB00005B/2264